MAKING IT HAPPEN

Studying Organizations:
Innovations in Methodology

PROJECT ON INNOVATIONS IN METHODOLOGY
FOR STUDYING ORGANIZATIONS

Project Planning Committee

Thomas J. Bouchard, *University of Minnesota*
Joel T. Campbell, *Educational Testing Service*
David L. DeVries, *Center for Creative Leadership*
J. Richard Hackman (Chair), *Yale University*
Joseph L. Moses, *American Telephone and Telegraph Company*
Barry M. Staw, *University of California, Berkeley*
Victor H. Vroom, *Yale University*
Karl E. Weick, *Cornell University*

Project Sponsorship and Administration

The volumes in this series (listed above) are among the products of a multi-year project on innovations in methodology for organizational research, sponsored by Division 14 (Industrial and Organizational Psychology) of the American Psychological Association.

Support for the project was provided jointly by the Organizational Effectiveness Research Program of the Office of Naval Research (Bert T. King, Scientific Officer), and by the School Management and Organizational Studies Unit of the National Institute of Education (Fritz Mulhauser, Scientific Officer). The central office of the American Psychological Association contributed its services for the management of project finances.

Technical and administrative support for the project was provided by the Center for Creative Leadership (Greensboro, NC) under the direction of David L. DeVries and Ann M. Morrison.

STUDYING
ORGANIZATIONS:
Innovations
in Methodology

3

MAKING IT HAPPEN

DESIGNING RESEARCH WITH IMPLEMENTATION IN MIND

by
**Milton D. Hakel, Melvin Sorcher,
Michael Beer,** and **Joseph L. Moses**

Published in cooperation with Division 14 of the
AMERICAN PSYCHOLOGICAL ASSOCIATION

SAGE PUBLICATIONS
Beverly Hills / London / New Delhi

For information address:

SAGE Publications, Inc.
275 South Beverly Drive
Beverly Hills, California 90212

SAGE Publications India Pvt. Ltd.
C-236 Defence Colony
New Delhi 110 024, India

SAGE Publications Ltd
28 Banner Street
London EC1Y 8QE, England

Printed in the United States of America

Library of Congress Cataloging in Publication Data

Main entry under title:

Making it happen.

    (Studying organizations : innovations in
methodology ; v. 3)
    "Published in cooperation with Division 14 of
the American Psychological Association."
    Bibliography: p.
    1. Organizational research. 2. Psychological research.
I. *Hakel*, Milton D. II. American Psychological
Association. Division of Industrial-Organizational
Psychology. III. Series: Studying organizations ; v. 3.
HD30.4.M34 1982   001.4'2   82-10726
ISBN 0-8039-1866-6 pbk.

FIRST PRINTING

Contents

Preface

There has been increasing interest in recent years, both in academia and in society at large, in how—and how well—organizations function. Educational, human service, political, and work organizations all have come under close scrutiny by those who manage them, those who work in them, and those who are served by them. The questions that have been raised are important ones. How, for example, can organizations become leaner (and, in many cases, smaller) as the birthrate and the rate of economic growth decline? Is there a trade-off between organizational productivity and the quality of life at work? Or can life at work and productivity be simultaneously improved? What changes in organizational practices are required to increase the career mobility of traditionally disadvantaged groups in society? How are we to understand the apparent asynchrony between the goals of educational organizations and the requirements of work organizations? How can public services be provided more responsively and with greater cost effectiveness? What new and nondiscriminatory devices can be developed to test, assess, and place people in schools and in industry? The list goes on, and it is long.

Unfortunately, there is reason for concern about our capability to build a systematic base of knowledge that can be used to deal with questions such as these. Available strategies for

studying organizations have emerged more or less indepen-
dently from a variety of disciplines, ranging from anthropology,
sociology, and political science to educational, industrial, and
organizational psychology. But none of these disciplines
appears to be on the verge of generating the kind of knowledge
about organizations that will be required to understand them
in their full richness and complexity.

Why not? Part of the problem may have to do with the
restrictiveness of discipline-based research—that is, the tendency of academic disciplines to support specific and focused
research paradigms, and to foster intense but narrow study of
particular and well-defined research "topics." Another possibility, however, is that the *methodologies* used in research on
organizations have been far too limited and conventional.

In general, the methods used in studying organizations have
been imported from one or another of the academic disciplines.
And while these methods may be fully appropriate for the
particular research problems and paradigms that are dominant
in the disciplines from which they come, they also may blind
those who use them to potentially significant new findings and
insights about how organizations operate.

Because the need for higher quality organizational research
is pressing, now may be the time to try to break through the
constraints of traditional methodologies and seek new
approaches to organizational research. This was the thinking
of the Executive Committee of Division 14 (Industrial and
Organizational Psychology) of the American Psychological
Association when, a few years ago, it initiated a project
intended to foster innovations in methodology for organizational research. A planning committee was appointed, and
support was obtained from the Office of Naval Research and
the National Institute of Education. Eighteen scholars were
recruited from a variety of disciplines and formed into six
working groups to review the state of organizational research
methodologies, and to seek innovative approaches to under-

standing organizations. A three-day conference was held at the Center for Creative Leadership, at which about sixty organizational researchers (representing a variety of disciplinary orientations, and from applied as well as academic settings) reviewed the findings and proposals of the six working groups. The working groups then revised their materials based on the reactions of conference participants, and the six monographs in this series are the result.

The content of the six monographs is wide ranging, from new quantitative techniques for analyzing data to alternative ways of gathering and using qualitative data about organizations. From "judgment calls" in designing research on organizations, to ways of doing research that encourage the *implementation* of the research findings. From innovative ways of formulating research questions about organizations to new strategies for cumulating research findings across studies.

This monograph focuses specifically on designing and executing research when one aspires to *implementation* of the findings. It turns out that textbook rules for the conduct of research often compromise the likelihood that research findings will actually be used in the organization in which the research is conducted. The authors offer numerous ideas and exercises (including one fully developed case of a research project in which hoped-for implementation did *not* happen) to help readers learn how to conduct research that can make a constructive difference in organizational life.

The aspiration of the numerous people who contributed their time and talent to the innovations project (they are listed facing the title page) is that readers of this monograph—and of its companions in the series—will discover here some ideas about methods that can be used to benefit both the quality and the usefulness of their own research on organizations.

—*J. Richard Hackman*
Series Editor

Acknowledgments

☐ We express our gratitude to Virginia Boehm and Personnel Psychology, Inc., for permission to reprint "Research in the 'Real World'—A Conceptual Model," and Andrew M. Pettigrew and Plenum Publishing Co., for permission to reprint "Towards a Political Theory of Organizational Intervention, published in *Human Relations*, Vol. 28(3), pages 191-208.

Introduction

☐ This monograph is intended both for new researchers and established researchers. It may be used as a means of stimulating personal reflection and evaluation, and as a text in a course. The monograph and the workshop that preceded it are the products of a vigorous collaboration. Spirited debates preceded the development of the overall plan of the book and the construction of each of the original products contained in it. Joel Moses, with assistance from Bob Lorenzo, developed the Research Style Inventory. Mike Beer developed the Comp Graf case, and Mel Sorcher developed the implementation role plays. Milt Hakel provided editorial guidance. In a way, each of these contributions reflects our own dominant orientation. Perhaps they illustrate the Law of the Hammer: once one has a hammer, it is amazing how many things are found that need pounding. Each of us has a different hammer and we have brought them to bear on this book. Moses has penchant for data collection leading to high-impact communications. Beer emphasizes knowing and understanding, and as a consequence vigorously advocates the case method both at Harvard and elsewhere. Sorcher's forte is doing things effectively, as illustrated in his development of Applied Learning, but in this case due to limited time and resources, his "hammer" is limited to role play, just one component of Applied Learning. Hakel likes to analyze and mull over issues. These hammers—data, knowledge, action, and reflection—have been brought to bear on research and implementation with the hope that researchers will use all of them.

While each of us will continue to emphasize his favorite tools and viewpoints, we are convinced that the product of our collaborative effort is more than the mere sum of the parts. Doing scientific research is a social venture—a venture that is strengthened by collaboration and review. Moreover, today's knowledge will be revised and superseded by tomorrow's research and theories. In this dynamic context a book can be a frightfully static thing. We have not sought to provide answers, however, but rather to raise issues about research and implementation that require continued scrutiny.

There is a history of science and a sociology of science. Occasionally, there are hints about a psychology of science. But as yet there is no science of science. Doing scientific research effectively involves technique, craft, and art. Appreciation and application of scientific research, artful in its execution, is something that we prize as behavioral scientists.

We have developed this monograph with two objectives. At an immediate focus, these materials are intended to illustrate key behaviors and key constraints in designing and doing research and implementation. At an ultimate focus, our objective is to encourage you to make bold research contributions to tangible problems.

—*M.D.H.*
—*M. S.*
—*M. B.*
—*J.L.M.*

1

Doing Research
and Implementation

☐ People do research for many different purposes. If you should happen to interview a collection of researchers, you would find a great diversity of opinion about the proper purposes and motives for doing research. Some do research to test theories, and some seek promotion, tenure, fame, and fortune. Some do it for its intrinsic interest. Others do it to solve practical problems.

Our concern is research *and* implementation. While a great deal of this text could be devoted to an interesting and worthwhile examination of the purposes for doing research and the motivational dynamics of researchers, our focus is much more specific.

Doing research entails considering a large set of issues—selecting and conceptualizing the problem, designing and executing the data collection, analyzing and interpreting the results, extending the design to follow interesting leads, and so on. Doing implementation entails another large set of issues—identifying and diagnosing the problem, gaining sponsorship and resources, setting goals and developing procedures, handling interpersonal "politics," producing results, and the like. This monograph focuses on the intersection of these two sets. It concerns both research and implementation, not issues unique to one or to the other. In applied science fields such as industrial and organization psychology, there are vast differences of opinion about what constitutes proper scientific and professional practice. Some researchers seem to hold an opinion that there is a world of difference in quality between research done in accord with proper scientific standards and applied research. Useful research, that is, research that offers the promise of immediate benefit to someone in solving a practical problem, is viewed as effort that is unlikely to generate scientific knowledge. Taken to its extreme, this view seems to suggest that science and application are antithetical, an obvious absurdity. But backing off from the extreme, the need is to occupy the middle ground, that is, to design implementation projects that also yield gains in scientific knowledge and to design scientific research that also yields applied programs and products. The concept of equifinality applies here—there are many means by which basic and applied goals might be attained. And they might be attained jointly.

Many issues need attention. What *is* the proper balance between an emphasis on pure/basic research and applied problem solving? To what extent *should* research subjects participate in the design, conduct, and sponsorship of research? To what extent *may* researchers take advocacy stands on issues? Who owns the products of scientists' efforts? What rights do research sponsors have?

The research process has been described as the most significant development in social behavior since the invention of representative government. Research is a social process, and a continuing probe of one's positions with respect to the research and implementation issues noted above is an important activity. New researchers need to face the issues at the outset of their research careers and established researchers need to reexamine them as their careers advance. In raising these issues, our ultimate objective is to encourage researchers to make *bold research contributions to tangible problems.*

Think about the key words italicized above—bold as opposed to timid, cautious, or safe. Research as opposed to speculation. Contribution as opposed to disservice or detriment. Tangible instead of tenuous, and problem instead of minutium.

Such an objective will not be achieved by merely reading this book. We have therefore set an additional but more modest

objective which, if achieved, will facilitate achievement of the ultimate objective. Our immediate objective is to illustrate *key behaviors* and *key constraints in designing research and implementation.*
One's own behavior and opinions are often useful starting points in exploring a set of issues. In the case of doing research and implementation, there are many viewpoints on many issues and the Research Style Inventory presents a useful way to guage your starting point.

RESEARCH STYLE INVENTORY

Check *True* if the statement is characteristic of most of your own research. Check *False* if the statement usually does not apply or is not generally true. If you have not yet done research, respond in terms of how you would handle your first project.

	True	False
(1) In preparing to present research proposals/results to management, I refrain from "packaging" my material in an impressive fashion, but rather I let the ideas speak for themselves.	___	___
(2) I can anticipate the actual benefits to a sponsoring organization before initiating a research project with it.	___	___
(3) Before presenting research proposals/results to management, I attempt to determine whether I am communicating with the proper audience, i.e., those managers with the power and ability to help put my ideas into action.	___	___

(4) When contacting members of the client organization, I do my best to come across as an expert.

     _____   _____

(5) When formulating a research plan, I try to involve managers in planning the actual research design.

     _____   _____

(6) In presenting a research proposal to management, I indicate that I have already determined the optimal design of "game plan" for conducting the research.

     _____   _____

(7) In presenting research proposals/results to management, I tend to adopt a scientific rather than practical orientation.

     _____   _____

(8) In designing research, I expect that the assignment of participants to experimental and control groups may have detrimental effects on the functioning of the participants.

     _____   _____

(9) Although it is very interesting from a theoretical and/or methodological standpoint, the research I design and conduct often has no real impact on the future functioning of the participating organization.

     _____   _____

(10) Quite often I can anticipate ill will and hostility occurring between/among management and the participants as a product of their receiving negative feedback from me.

     _____   _____

(11) In designing research, I would allow for the possibility that part or all of my research could be "piggy-backed" onto a project or projects in which the participants are

     _____   _____

already involved but that are of no real interest to me.

(12) I often can anticipate that my research will require a considerable expenditure of time and/or expense on the part of persons who cannot afford it (they have better things to do).

     _____ _____

(13) In preparing to conduct research, I usually refrain from determining the extent to which the client organization could provide technical support for my project.

     _____ _____

(14) In designing research, I would allow for the possibility that some issues that management has been meaning to investigate can be incorporated into my research.

     _____ _____

(15) If I were to design and conduct a field experiment, the experimental and control groups would be naturally occurring or could be easily created.

     _____ _____

(16) In designing research I would do my best to allow the participants (subjects) to gain from their experiences in the project.

     _____ _____

(17) In designing research, I often anticipate that I might have to provide potentially sensitive information regarding research participants to other participants and/or management.

     _____ _____

(18) In designing research, I would attempt to give meaningful information to management and the

     _____ _____

participants relatively soon after the initiation of the intervention or in "stages" as the data collection/analyses progress.

(19) In designing research, I would do my best to ensure that the withholding of treatment from a control group would not cause feelings of inequity or other dysfunctional consequences.

    _____   _____

(20) In designing research, I would take steps to ensure that, should it be necessary to present negative feedback to management or the participants, it could be done in such a fashion that it would be interpreted as constructive criticism.

    _____   _____

(21) If at all possible, I would design research that would have the potential to develop into or suggest an ongoing process of some benefit to the participating organization.

    _____   _____

SCORING KEY AND INTERPRETATION GUIDE

Few of the items in the Research Style Inventory have universally correct answers. Providing a scoring key and interpretation guide makes sense, therefore, only as a means of exploring the meanings of the items. Many of the items involve conflicting viewpoints and raise issues that need discussion. The purpose of discussion should be to find proper balance points for handling the issues, rather than to defend one or another answer as the "correct" one.

The keyed answers represent our judgment based on assumptions about typical situations involving research being done with implementation in mind.

(1) *False.* Although attractive packaging (e.g., quality printing and binding of written material, use of multicolor flip charts and/or slides) is purely a question of cosmetics and certainly can not compensate for shoddy research design, an impressive presentation conveys to managers that the project is a worthwhile investment.

(2) *True.* Managers need to know "what's in it" for them. While you will not be able to guess *all* of the benefits of a project, let alone the consequences, you need to identify the major ones.

(3) *True.* Building a constituency for the project is important, and without the support of powerful, able managers, support from others gives little advantage in pursuing the project.

(4) *False.* The "expert syndrome" should be avoided since (a) it creates a needless gap between management and the would-be researcher, and (b) it presumes that the researcher has all the answers, an expectation that is unlikely to be fulfilled. Of course, establishing one's credibility is important, but that is not done well by making others feel inadequate.

(5) *True.* Here again, expertise is an underlying issue. Getting a manager involved in planning a research design is a far cry from delegating that activity to managers. And many managers will want to have a say in the development and execution of the research plan, regardless of their expertise. Denying this involvement will have consequences later.

(6) *False.* This would discourage managers from offering potentially valuable information/recommendations of their own and would limit the extent to which they could experience a sense of involvement in the project.

(7) *False.* Nothing can turn a group of managers off more quickly than a lecture by a scientist.

(8) *False.* If this is the case, you should try to be more flexible and creative in your approach to designing research (for example, you might try to identify naturally occurring experimental and control groups.)

(9) *False*. Few organizations are willing to invest time and expense in a project from which they will not somehow benefit.

(10) *False*. Besides the obvious ethical implications, chances are some of the more astute managers in your audience will also pick up on this possibility and will not wish to participate.

(11) *True*. Internal and external validity are essential for scientific progress, and so are the material resources represented by an organization's participation in the research. Here is an instance in which a judgment call is necessary, and many studies could be successfully "piggybacked."

(12) *False*. If this is the case, perhaps you should consider narrowing the scope of your proposed research in the hope that interesting/ useful results will entice management to participate in one or more additional projects in the future. Alternatively, you could reevaluate your choice of that particular organization as a research setting, if possible.

(13) *False*. If this is the case, you might be mildly surprised to discover that certain individuals or units in the host organization would be able and would even enjoy the opportunity to assist you, especially if they (or their superiors) view their involvement in the research as a potential learning experience.

(14) *True*. This is another facet of the issue addressed in item 11—can multiple purposes be served in one research design? Management interest will add to support for the study.

(15) *True*. Using intact groups creates a design tradeoff and feasibility has to be a prime criterion in selecting a specific design for a field experiment.

(16) *True*. Ethical principles and research regulations control the extent to which research participants should be exposed to risk of harm or loss, and differential gain is also an issue. But gain should always be preferred to loss.

(17) *False*. Again, in addition to ethical considerations, managers may react negatively to having sensitive information regarding certain employees made known to others (although they might be eager to obtain such information themselves).

(18) *True*. Quick feedback is essential for maintaining participant (and sponsor) interest. Of course, internal validity needs to be safeguarded in sequential designs.

(19) *True.* Managers and research participants understand the need for control to ensure valid research conclusions, and differential gain can be a tough issue to resolve. After the experiment ends, equity needs to be restored.

(20) *True.* The skill and grace with which negative feedback is given has major implications for the continuation of the research project and for future researchers.

(21) *True.* If the objective is "research *and* implementation," this answer is obvious.

ISSUES TO THINK ABOUT AND TALK OVER WITH COLLEAGUES

(1) What are the advantages of involving participants in the design and execution of research? What are the disadvantages?

(2) Gaining authorization to conduct research, gaining cooperation in doing research, and implementing programs or procedures based on research results require the researcher to communicate persuasively. To what extent to scientists' ethics limit them in making value judgments? In advocating specific programs or views? In "selling" their services? Should scientists' ethics differ from commercial ethics in the matter of selling basic research? In selling research that leads to implementation?

(3) Cost/benefit analysis and accountability enjoy current prominence in discussions of funding for basic and applied research. To what extent should the source of the funding (the sponsor) have influence on the design and execution of basic research? Applied research? Program or product development? To what extent should the sponsor exclusively enjoy the benefits of basic research? Applied research? Program or product development?

PLAN OF THE BOOK

The Research Style Inventory has served to raise several issues that pervade the practice of research for implementation, and they receive scrutiny going from the abstract to the concrete in the following chapters. The next two chapters deal with the general context in which organizational research is done. First, Virginia Boehm deals in Chapter 2 with some stereotypes about the way in which research is conducted in organizations. Then, in Chapter 3 Andrew Pettigrew calls our attention to the political issues of intervention. These two chapters provide a general framework for understanding how to proceed when doing research for implementation.

Chapter 4 tests that understanding concretely in the confines of a specific situation. The Comp Graf case study offers an opportunity to apply the insights derived from discussing the Research Style Inventory and from studying Boehm's and Pettigrew's contributions. In addition, it draws on the specific context of the company and knowledge of job stress.

Chapter 5 moves us from concepts to action, and presents the most stringent test of skill. Role plays, representing typical problem situation in negotiating with managers and persuading others to support a research project, provide the stimulus for practice and feedback on handling research and implementation issues in real time. The final chapter summarizes the issues and offers implications for the conduct of research and implementation.

2

Doing Research in the "Real World"

☐ The research process in the social sciences has been described by many authors. Study of the process is a key ingredient in many graduate and undergraduate courses. The chances are high that you are familiar with standard research designs, with deriving hypotheses from theory or from the literature, and with many data analysis methods. Much of our research apparatus is modeled from the physical and biological sciences. Deduction and theory testing serve as precedents which we in the social sciences try to emulate.

The following article by Virginia Boehm offers another perspective on the research process. It is a provocative description of experienced "realities" in the "real world" of applied research in organizations.

Given the vigor with which scientists have pursued other phenomena, it is odd that so little attention has been paid to the scientific description and explanation of the research process itself. Which of Boehm's models offers the best prospect for gaining insight into the art of doing scientific research?

Research in the "Real World"—A Conceptual Model

Virginia R. Boehm

The Standard Oil Company (Ohio)

Research in Industrial/Organizational Psychology has been primarily based on a traditional model of scientific inquiry developed as an outgrowth of research in the physical sciences. The premise of this paper is that this traditional model of research frequently does not fit the realities of applied I/O research in "real world" settings and, when pursued exclusively, operates to limit progress in the field. An alternative research model, based on the realities of "what is," rather than on the ideal of "what should be" is proposed, and examples of lines of inquiry where this alternative model might have utility are provided. The traditional and alternative models are viewed as mutually supportive and jointly capable of producing advances in I/O psychology which cannot be achieved by either method in isolation.

Industrial/Organizational psychology, along with other data-based social sciences, shares with physical science a basic method-

AUTHOR'S NOTE: *An earlier version of this paper was presented at the meeting of the Eastern Psychological Association, Washington, D.C., April, 1978. Requests for reprints should be sent to Virginia R. Boehm, 1521 Midland Building, Cleveland, Ohio 44115.*

ology—the "scientific method." This mode of inquiry incorporates some basic principles of the scientific method involving such concepts as the "null hypothesis" and "type one and type two error," and an empirical data-based tradition.

Industrial/Organizational psychology (I/O) is also a field being investigated both by academically-oriented psychologists working in university settings and psychologists employed by business and industry.

The central theme of this paper is that I/O, as a field, can best advance when the contributions of the academic and empirical approaches are combined, and that this is most likely to occur when the differences in the applicable research models in these two settings are mutually recognized and respected.

The traditional academic model of the scientific method in psychology has frequently been explicated and (in a simplified version) is expressed in Figure 2.1.

To quickly review, an area of investigation is selected, a topic is refined, based on prior research, and a study is conducted. This research (at least academically) follows a historically determined model: Hypotheses are formulated, a study is designed to test them, the study is conducted and statistical knowledge utilized to analyze the results.

Where the hypotheses and results mesh, good. Where they don't, internal (or post-hoc) analyses are conducted to account for this, and/or hypotheses are revised in view of the results. The "by the book" model presented here is over-simplified, but it does reflect the underlying principle of taking an idea and logically following it step-by-step to the point where the null hypotheses are rejected or not.

Realistically, it is generally recognized that things are more complex in practice. Some hypotheses work out, some don't, so internal analyses are performed that were not initially planned; after a study has been conducted, it seems clear that there is an alternative explanation of the results that the initial design does not permit ruling out; something happens during the conduct of

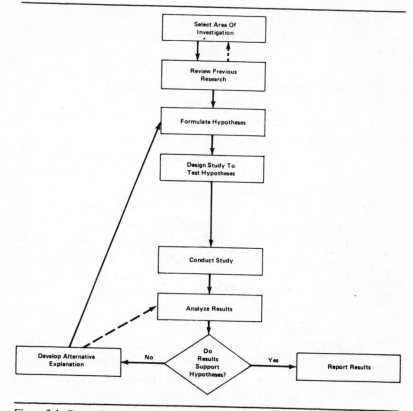

Figure 2.1 Research Process "By the Book"

the study that introduces unplanned and unwanted variance, etc. But, in theory, this is the model of the scientific method and it is a model that has greatly benefited the progress of science, particularly the physical sciences.

However, when attempts are made to utilize this model in "real world" settings (as in-house I/O psychologists or as consultants to organizations) it very rapidly becomes apparent that there is a disparity between the "state of the science" in I/O psychology and the "state of the art" regarding application of behavioral science principles to organizational reality.

However, to a greater or lesser degree, the traditional model of scientific inquiry has been accepted as an ideal, even by "real world" researchers who find themselves operating in an environment which is quite different, and which leads to a different process of scientific inquiry. The organizational research process might be conceptualized something like this:

The level of oversimplification involved in Figure 2.2 is analogous to that shown in the "by the book" model in Figure 2.1.

But, the most casual comparison of the models indicates three striking differences: (1) The number of processes involved in the "what is" organizational model is greater than the number in the "what should be" scientific model; (2) The interactions between the stages in the models are more numerous and complex for the organizational model; and (3) The focus of inquiry shifts from the scientific quest to learn what the facts are to an organizational need to solve a current or anticipated performance problem. That the overcoming or avoidance of a performance deficiency is the motive for undertaking organizational research efforts has been recognized elsewhere (Gilbert, 1978).

In short, the "what is" model is, scientifically, distinctly messy in terms of methodology, complexity, statistical analysis, and the conclusions that can be drawn. Yet, at the same time, it seems to present a more accurate picture of organizational reality than a model based on "what should be."

While there have been, particularly in the area of evaluation research, acknowledgements that "nonscientific" considerations have strong impacts on the conduct of organizational research (Weiss, 1975), rather ingenious attempts to circumvent these factors via experimental design (Cook & Campbell, 1976), and acknowledgement that these considerations may adversely impact scientific growth and communication (Latane, 1978), criticisms have come from the perspective of altering or taking into account environmental circumstances, rather than revising the model of inquiry. By and large, the reaction of behavioral scientists, when faced by the realities of the organizational

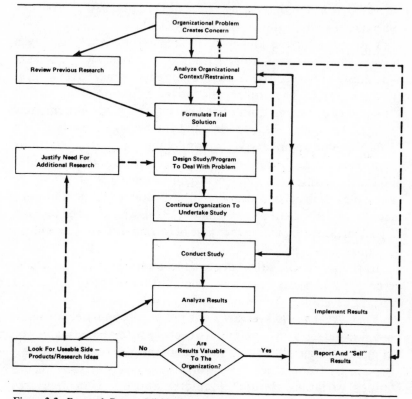

Figure 2.2 Research Process Within Organizations

research environment, has been either to attempt modification of
the environment to fit the traditional mode of inquiry or else to
opt out of the scientific establishment.

We go through procrustean convolutions to make the environmental circumstances under which we work at least marginally
compatible with the traditional model. For example, we labor
vigorously to achieve the experimental ideal of random assignment to experimental and control groups, we develop statistical
techniques to deal with restriction of range, we fight administrative battles to prevent predictor scores from influencing
criterion measures, etc. In short, behavioral scientists in "real

world" settings undertake a variety of Quixotic battles designed to make the environment fit the model.

Why not alter the model to fit the environment? And, even within the constraints of the traditional model, why not take advantage of the positive features of the environment of organizational research? The primary dictionary definition of "model" is "a small copy or imitation of an existing object" (Webster's New World Dictionary, 1959, p. 945) but the "scientific method" is a reflection of a secondary Webster's definition, "a person or thing considered as a standard of excellence to be imitated." The idea that the traditional model of organizational research may be alterable and in need of alteration was mentioned tangentially in a recent article by Daft and Wiginton (1979), who referred to ". . . a trickle of doubt regarding the value of certain styles of research on organizations" (p. 180).

Insistence on sole adherence to a secondary definition of what a model should be can be viewed as having limited the advancement of I/O psychology in four ways:

First, "real world" research has not been adequately disseminated in the scientific community because such research is viewed as methodologically flawed. In terms of the traditional model this is perfectly true—much "real world" research is messy—uncontrolled variables abound, predictor and criterion measures interact, alternative hypotheses cannot be ruled out; standard statistical procedures cannot be applied without massive violation of assumptions. While other factors aside from methodological "problems" play a role in this lack of dissemination—differences in the reward systems for academic and organizational psychologists and the proprietary nature of some types of organizational research—the primary reason for adequate dissemination is methodological inadequacy under the standards of the traditional model.

That such methodological "imprecision" may be an accurate reflection of the organizational environment and, in fact, a desirable characteristic has been pointed out only rarely (i.e.,

Daft & Wiginton, 1979). Also, only occasionally have the circumstances that lead to these (in traditional terms) methodological "difficulties" been explicated in published research. One notable example was a study by Locke, Sirota, and Wolfson (1976) dealing with the successes and failures of job enrichment. Another study (Mobley, Hand, Baker, & Meglino, 1979) indicates that a complex and multi-dimensional model may be needed to accurately predict organizational choice.

Secondly, academic research has not been maximally incorporated into the day-to-day functioning of organizations. Practitioners have frequently discounted what academic researchers have discovered because the traditional model does not fit the practitioner's reality and because findings are stated in terms that the practitioner cannot translate into saleable organizational policy. For example, the topic of goal setting has been extensively studied. How much of this knowledge is utilized by I/O practitioners establishing and evaluating MBO programs in organizations?

When the attempt to incorporate academic research into organizations has occurred, less than adequate consideration of organizational realities has led to unexpected results. For example, the frequently cited Pedalino and Gamboa (1974) study of the use of behavior modification to improve attendance was a scientific success, but not an organizational one. The lottery incentive introduced proved extremely popular with the workers whose behavior was being modified and had to be discontinued so it would not become an issue in labor negotiations!

The third problem is that, to a substantial extent the traditional model of research has dictated the kinds of problems investigated. Since the organizational environment presents such great problems in the conduct of research using the traditional model, there is a tendency to limit investigation to those areas where it is at least possible to conduct investigations that more or less conform to the model. This results in avoidance of the really messy areas— i.e., evaluating management training and development using on-the-job performance measures or cost/benefit analysis; investigating the impact of organizational staffing policies and procedures on employee productivity or satisfaction; studying the effects of "outside" interventions such as EEO and OSHA on the productivity of organizational units. Published research in these areas is sparse, and yet it is in these areas where opportunities to achieve maximum organizational impact and change, based on behavioral science foundations, are greatest. These are the "hotspots" having direct bearing on the bottom-line profitability of organizations.

Finally, because research efforts are viewed in terms of the traditional model of inquiry, there is a tendency to overlook the *positive* features of conducting research in the organizational environment. Moving from one model of inquiry to the other involves a series of trade-offs. On the balance, this series of trade-offs demonstrates the value of both traditional research and "real world" research. Some of the relevant trade-offs are these (see Figure 2.3):

The characteristics of traditional and organizational research vary all along the line, starting with their basic orientation. The academic psychologist seeks to investigate an issue or test a theoretical concept. The "real world" psychologist seeks an answer to (or at least an explanation of) an organizational problem. The difference here makes it easy for academics and practitioners to pin labels on one another—"Ivory tower types," "Dust-bowl empiricists."

But, in fact, the difference between academic theory-generated research and "real world" research-generated theory provides an opportunity for extremely valuable cross-fertilization in both areas—opportunities that have not been maximally utilized.

In areas where this cross-fertilization has taken place, advances have been rapid. For example, organizational studies of how careers unfold in organizations (e.g., Bray, Campbell, & Grant, 1974) have led to the beginnings of theory and model-building in this area (Hall, 1976). Very pragmatic organizational studies of the comparative validity of selection tests for Blacks and Whites

Research Characteristic	Give Up	Gain
Basic Orientation	Theory Generates Research	Research Generates Theory
Topic Of Inquiry	Freedom To Pursue Obstruse (But Interesting) Lines Of Inquiry	Direct Organizational (And Sometimes Societal) Impact
Experimental Design	Use Of Complex Factorial Paradigms	Capacity For Repeated Measures And Longitudinal Studies
Sample Investigated	Control Over Precise Sample Composition	Ability To Define And Investigate Population
Interpretation Of Results	Exclusion Of Alternative Hypotheses	Increased Generalizability

Figure 2.3   Trade-Offs Involved in Research in Organizations

have led to numerous statistical models of test fairness and to methodological advances in the area of validity generalization (Schmidt & Hunter, 1977).

The design trade-off is another one where profitable cross-fertilization is possible. One area is the evaluation of multiple interventions aimed at improving worker performance. A recent study (Bourdon, 1977) was aimed at dealing with an organizational problem—poor managerial performance—using a type of multiple base-line longitudinal design (a design better suited to organizational than academic research). Multiple interventions were utilized simultaneously—formal training, goal setting, a token economy point system, feedback, and social reinforcers. The design used allowed a conclusive demonstration that something worked. But which of these procedures or what set of interactions between them was effective cannot be determined from this design. Such a determination requires a highly complex factorial design, virtually impossible in an organizational environment, but made-to-order for a university laboratory.

These issues also influence the interpretation of research results. Reviewing the organizational model in Figure 2.2, it seems apparent that the interactions between the components are such that, in a given study, the number of opportunities for "Murphy's Law" to operate are enormous. Very occasionally these interactions will facilitate obtaining positive results but mostly they will interfere by introducing substantial amounts of "error variance" into the data. If, in spite of the problems, positive results are obtained, the finding is very likely to be a replicable one in the more controlled laboratory environment. The reverse is not the case.

Finally, the organizational model suggests some design possibilities to the investigator. For example, if, as the model suggests, the conduct of the study and the organizational context can be *expected* to interact, why not build this anticipated interaction into the design of the study and measure it? This has been suggested by Komaki (1977) as a strategy in evaluation research and is equally applicable to other areas the I/O psychologist may investigate in organizational settings.

Along the same lines, the model suggests areas where methodological advances are needed. For example, Cook and Campbell (1976) point out that "In particular, no adequate statistical tests yet exist for the most frequently used quasi-experimental design in which nonequivalent groups, whose pretest performance levels vary, receive different treatments" (p. 232). Rather than trying to circumvent situations of this type (which simply cannot be done given the problem-solving orientation of the organizational research model) let's learn how to handle them. The probability that organizational reality can be revised to conform with behavioral science principles is near zero. What is needed are research techniques aimed at making behavioral science findings more organizationally applicable. Further development of statistical techniques for time-series experiments (Simonton, 1977) would appear to be one promising line of inquiry.

Organizations do not exist primarily as research laboratories for behavioral scientists. If this basic fact of life is recognized and a model based on "what is" is accepted as being as equally legitimate as the model of "what should be," there are exciting possibilities for the advancement of I/O psychology, both scientifically and empirically.

If, however, I/O psychologists continue to adhere solely to a model based on the ideal, in which organizational realities are viewed solely as problems to be circumvented, stagnation of the field is a strong possibility, and widening of the communications gap between academic and organizational I/O psychologists a virtual certainty.

REFERENCES

Bourdon, R. D. A token economy application to management performance improvement. *Journal of Organizational Behavior Management,* 1977, 1, 23-27.

Bray, D. W., Campbell, R. J., & Grant, D. L. *Formative years in business.* New York: John Wiley, 1974.

Cook, T. D., & Campbell, D. T. The design and conduct of quasi-experiments and true experiments in field settings. In M. D. Dunnette (Ed.), *Handbook of Industrial Organizational Psychology.* Chicago: Rand McNally, 1976.

Daft, R. L., & Wiginton, J. C. Language and organization. *Academy of Management Review,* 1979, 4, 179-191.

Gilbert, T. F. *Human competence.* New York: McGraw-Hill, 1978.

Hall, D. T. *Careers in organizations.* Pacific Palisades, CA: Goodyear, 1976.

Komaki, J. Alternative evaluation strategies in work settings: Reversal and multiple-baseline designs. *Journal of Organizational Behavior Management,* 1977, 1, 53-77.

Latane, B. Notes for a talk on our scientific publication system. *Personality and Social Psychology Bulletin,* 1978, 4, 22-23.

Locke, E. A., Sirota, D., & Wolfson, A. D. An experimental case study of the successes and failures of job enrichment in a government agency. *Journal of Applied Psychology,* 1976, 61, 701-711.

Mobley, W. H., Hand, H. H., Baker, R. L., & Meglino, B. M. Conceptual and empirical analysis of military recruit training attrition. *Journal of Applied Psychology,* 1979, 64, 10-18.

Pedalino, E., & Gamboa, V. U. Behavior Modification and absenteeism: Intervention in one industrial setting. *Journal of Applied Psychology,* 1974, 59, 694-698.

Schmidt, F. L., & Hunter, J. E. Development of a general solution to the problem of validity generalization. *Journal of Applied Psychology,* 1977, 62, 529-540.

Simonton, D. K. Cross-sectional time-series experiments: Some suggested statistical analysis. *Psychological Bulletin,* 1977, 84, 489-502.

Webster's New World Dictionary of the American Language (College Edition). Cleveland: World, 1959.

Weiss, C. H. Evaluation research in the political context. In E. L. Struening & M. Guttentag (Eds.), *Handbook of Evaluation Research* (Vol. 1). Beverly Hills, CA: Sage, 1975.

3

Politics, Motives, and Values in Research Interventions

◻ Research in organizations occurs in a political, social, and economic context. This certainly is not "news," but nevertheless this point is too often taken for granted, or worse yet, ignored. Experienced researchers tend to take the organizational context for granted—it is the "ground" upon which the "figure" of the research study is displayed. Our publication practices reinforce this figure dominance, for they focus on theories, methods, results, and concepts that are generalizable from one organization to the next.

Reading the research literature serves as a poor introduction of organizational research to new researchers because the political, social, economic, and organizational context surrounding the prosecution of the research study is seldom included in that literature. In the following article Andrew Pettigrew describes some of the political factors to be considered in intervening in organizations.

Towards a Political Theory of Organizational Intervention

Andrew M. Pettigrew

This paper discusses the neglected theme of the political context of the interventionist's work in terms of the client-consultant relationship and the consultant-consultant relationship. It is suggested that the internal consultant's ability to influence clients will be a function of his possession and tactical use of five power resources: expertise, control over information, political access and sensitivity, assessed stature and group support. Of these, the first three appear to be necessary but not sufficient conditions for consultant power. Once he has the political access and understanding, the consultant's ability to negotiate and persuade depends on his assessed stature with the appropriate figures in his political network.

INTRODUCTION

One of the themes noticeably absent from much of the writing on organizational change is the political context of the

AUTHOR'S NOTE: *Chris Argyris of Harvard University, Martin Evans of the University of Toronto and Derek Pugh of the London Graduate School of Business Studies have provided helpful comments and criticisms of an earlier draft of this paper. The author accepts responsibility for the views that prevail.*

Pettigrew, Andrew M. Towards a political theory of organizational intervention. *Human Relations,* Volume 28, Number 3, pages 191-208. Reprinted with the permission of the author and the publisher.

interventionist's work. As Rhenman (1973, p. 162) argues, with the possible exception of Jacques (1951) and Whyte and Hamilton (1964) 'there is seldom any mention of a consultant's influence on the political system or his relations with the formal power system' of the organization. That this subject is rarely discussed in academic papers does not detract from its importance to those who have to live with its effects. The choice of project area, the formation of the project team, the development of the assignment and its likely acceptance and implementation by the client are all key transactions bounded by political forces within the organization.

This paper addresses itself to the problems internal consultants have in influencing clients. The organization is here assumed to be a political system. Political processes evolve at the group level from the division of work in the organization and at the individual level from associated career, reward and status systems. Sub-units develop interests based on specialized functions and responsibilities; individual careers are bound up with the maintenance and dissolution of certain types of organizational activity and with the distribution of organizational resources. At various times claims are made by sub-units and individuals on scarce organizational resources. The scope of the claims is likely to be in a reflection of the sub-units' perception of the criticalness of the resources to its survival and development. The success of any claimant in furthering his interests will be a consequence of his ability to mobilize power for his demands.

It is the involvement of sub-units in such demand and support generating processes which constitutes the political dimension. Political behaviour is defined as behaviour by individuals or, in collective terms, sub-units within an organization, which makes a claim against the resource sharing system of the organization.

The kinds of resources up for redistribution may vary from situation to situation. They may be salaries, promotion opportunities, capital expenditure, new equipment, and control over people, information or new areas of a business.

Political activity in organizations tends to be particularly associated with change (Burns & Stalker, 1961; Pettigrew, 1973b). Since internal consultants are the initiators of many organizational changes their activities and plans are inextricably bound up with the politics of change. Major structural changes, or even the possibilities of them, have political consequences. Innovations are likely to threaten existing parts of the working community. New resources may be created and appear to fall within the jurisdiction of a department or individual who had previously not been a claimant in a particular area. This department or its principal representative may see this as an opportunity to increase his power, status and rewards in the organization. Others may see their interests threatened by the change, and needs for security or the maintenance of power may provide the impetus for resistance. In all these ways new political action is released and ultimately the existing distribution of power is endangered.

The above analysis has suggested that the consultant-client relationship takes place in the context of organization life where political activity is pervasive and real. Furthermore, the activities of internal consultants, especially in so far as they demand structural changes in organizations, will affect the current balance in the distribution of power and thereby involve both client and consultant in those political processes. If that involvement is not proactive, then it will be reactive, as the political behaviour of others acts as a constraint on the range of behaviour possible for both client and consultant. In this situation, as Bennis (1969) has suggested, if the consultant bases his approach on two sources of influence, truth and love, then it seems likely his plans will remain only dreams. While strategies of influence based on organization development norms may be 'appropriate under conditions of truth, trust, love and collaboration' (Bennis, 1969, p. 77), they may be much less appropriate under the political settings described elsewhere by this and other authors (Dalton, 1959; Crozier, 1964; Pettigrew, 1973b). Part of the 'valid and useful information' not covered in

Argyris' theory (1970, p. 17) yet required by the internal consultant is a knowledge of the political processes in his own organization and an awareness of how the particular projects he is working on relate to, and by implication, alter, those processes.

An additional contextual factor which can greatly constrain the internal consultant's interpretation of his role is the stress to which he is exposed. In setting out a rather different theory of intervention from the present one, Argyris (1970, p. 144) emphasizes the importance for the consultant's effectiveness of his ability accurately to perceive stressful reality. This would seem to be a critical yet relatively unexplored issue.

This paper suggests that a principal source of consultant ineffectiveness is their tendency to react to the stresses built into their role and to their relationship with their clients rather than to formulate a proactive strategy based on a full anticipated awareness of their and their clients' position in the political system of their organization. The second major source of internal consultant ineffectiveness stems from their apparent inability to present a unified political force within their organization in dealing with clients. Often major differences in values, work style and career interests disrupt consultancy units and leave clients bewildered about the range and quality of service they can expect. Such uncertainties reflect badly on the credibility of the consultant (Pettigrew, 1973b). It should be clear then that internal consultant effectiveness is a function of *two* interdependencies. Those between client and consultant and those between consultant and consultant. The nature of the latter relationship has very important consequences for the range of possible behaviour in the former. This point is rarely discussed in the literature on client-consultant relationships.

THE SOURCES AND USE OF CONSULTANT POWER

It should not be assumed from the preceding discussion that political processes in organizations act merely as constraints on consultant activities. In fact, the central theme of this paper is to indicate the political opportunities available to the internal consultant by discussing some of the sources and use of consultant power. As Bennis points out, this has been a neglected approach, 'there seems to be a fundamental deficiency in models of change associated with organization development. It systematically avoids the problem of power, of the politics of change' (1969, p. 78).

Those who do include concepts of power in their theory of changing cannot regard the use of power as a neutral, pervasive aspect of organizational life. Power strategies are discussed as being narrowly coercive. Thus Kotler (1972, p. 183) argues a change agent power strategy involves the use of 'agent controlled sanctions' and Zaltman et al. (1972, p. 271) indicate 'power strategies tend to be coercive in nature. They are those strategies in which force and/or the threat of force is used'. While Walton's (1965) description of power strategies is equally dominated by the threat-promise style of interaction he does see a genuine role for power in any theory of social change and recommends that an adequate power base is likely to be important in any attempt to produce attitudinal change.

What is lacking from all these theories of intervention is an attempt to specify likely sources of consultant power and the mechanisms by which such resources are tactically used within the consulting process. The present analysis seeks in part to deal with that deficiency in the literature.

Power is not an attribute possessed by someone in isolation. It is a relational phenomenon. Power is generated, maintained and lost in the context of relationships with others. A power relation is a causal relation between the preferences of an actor regarding an outcome and the outcome itself. Power involves the ability of an actor to produce outcomes consonant with his perceived interests.

Most actors have power only in certain domains of activity. The scope of their power is limited by their structural position in their organization. This is because the resources which form the base of an actor's power are differentially located by structural position. In this sense, the transferability of power across system boundaries is regarded as problematic.

Power resources, however, must not only be possessed by an actor, they must also be controlled by him. Bannester (1969, p. 386) makes this point succinctly: 'It is immaterial who owns the gun and is licensed to carry it; the question is, who has his finger on the trigger?' Control, however, may not be enough; there is also the issue of the skilful use of resources. The successful use of power is also a tactical problem. The most effective strategy may not always be to pull the trigger.

From this viewpoint, the analysis of organizational power requires some attempt to map out the distribution and use of resources and the ability of actors to produce outcomes consonant with their perceived interests. As we shall see, the main practical problem for the consultant is the movement through the stages of possessing, controlling and tactically exploiting the power resources he possesses. Some consultants are not aware of the potential power resources they do possess. Others are aware of the resources but can neither effectively control nor tactically use them. But what are some of these potential consultant power resources and how and why might they be used?

This writer's research on systems analysts, programmers and operations researchers indicated that there are at least five potential power resources available to the internal consultant (Pettigrew, 1968, 1972, 1973a, b). These are:

1. Expertise.
2. Control over information.
3. Political access and sensitivity.
4. Assessed stature.
5. Group support.

These resources are separated here for analytical clarity; they are, of course, empirically highly interdependent.

EXPERTISE

Singular possession of a valued area of technical competence is perhaps the most familiar source of consultant power. In an early study by this author, 70% of a sample of operations researchers felt they had an influence on company decision-making. Asked how they were able to do this, 55% said 'because we alone have the time and techniques to produce detailed and novel solutions to complex problems of planning.'

The notion of dependency is crucial to the analysis of expert power. Emerson (1962) supplies the initial exploration of dependency. Blau (1964, p. 118) interprets him as follows:

> By supplying services in demand to others, a person establishes power over them. If he regularly renders needed services they cannot readily obtain elsewhere, others become dependent on and obligated to him for these services unless they in turn can supply services to the former person that he needs. The power of one individual over another thus depends on the social alternatives or lack of them available to the subjected individual.

The power of consultants over clients is likely to be consequent on the amount of dependency in the relationship. The consultant can maintain a power position over clients as long as they are dependent on him for special skills and access to certain kinds of information. One way that consultants can generate such dependency is to manipulate the uncertainty surrounding their expertise. Crozier (1964) has described this process between engineers and their clients. Pettigrew (1973a) illustrates the same processes between programmers and stock controllers and between programmers and systems analysts in the same firm.

The power of the consultant is unlikely to be omnipotent even with the most technically uncertain problem. Clearly most dependency relationships will be a matter of degree. The relative centrality and substitutability (Hickson et al., 1971) of the consultant group is likely to vary over time. In times of financial stringency the accountant's activities may become more central to the organization's survival. In times of the proliferation of consultant groups all operating from a similar task environment, one group's activities may be seen by client groups to be readily substitutable for another. One strategy used by clients to weaken consultant power is to create another source of consultant expertise and encourage competition between the two sources. External consultants may be brought in for this purpose. In both these situations dependency relationships may be difficult to generate and maintain.

CONTROL OVER INFORMATION

Several authors have mentioned the control over information as a power resource. Mechanic (1962) has argued within organizations dependency can be generated with others by controlling access to the resources of information, persons and instrumentalities. Burns and Stalker (1961) assert that information may become an instrument for advancing, attacking, or defending status. Using the prison as a setting, McCleery (1960) is able to demonstrate how the formal system of authority relations may be considerably modified by the location and control of communication channels. Because all reports had to pass through the custodial hierarchy this group was able to subvert the industrial and reform goals represented by the Prison Professional Services and Industry programs. The head of the custodial hierarchy, the prison captain, for the same reasons was able to exert considerable control over decisions made by his immediate superior, the warden.

This author's research (Pettigrew, 1972) indicates that the structural location of many internal consultants offers them particular advantage with regard to the control over organizational communications. Most internal consultants have roles with high boundary relevance (Khan et al., 1964). They have many significant work contacts across departmental boundaries within their own organization and between that organization and relevant others. In this regard, they are well positioned to take on the role of technical gate-keepers. As such they are potentially able to influence the resource allocation process in their organization through a process of collecting, filtering and reformulating information.

Previous research (Pettigrew, 1972, 1973b) has indicated consultant gate-keepers may be particularly effective at controlling information in the uncertain conditions surrounding innovative decisions. During these decisions, strategies of uncertainty absorption (March & Simon, p. 166) may enable consultants to produce outcomes in line with their perceived interests. Counter-biasing by clients in these decisions is likely to be problematic. In the consultant-client relationship where the information passed will be complex, uncertain and rapidly changing, the possibility for clients either to identify bias, or deal with it by counter-biasing, is likely to be that much more difficult.

Aside from their ability as gate-keepers to control the flow of technical information, consultants may have access to other sorts of information which they may be able to put to use. As part of their investigations into other departments, consultants may uncover the inefficiencies and incompetences of others. Even if they do not actually reveal these ineffiencies, the client may perceive the consultant has this information. Some consultants are prepared to use this information against recalcitrant clients. It is frequently referred to as the 'dirty linen strategy.'

The sole reliance on expert power through the demonstration of technical competence is rarely successful against a client probably already very defensive about his own lack of technical expertise. Baker and Schaffer (1969, p. 66) argue that inadequate client-consultant relationships are often made worse 'by the behaviour of the staff consultants, who mask their own unsureness and anxiety with a thick amount of professional jargon and technical talk.'

Few internal consultants can afford therefore to rely exclusively on their expertise and control of information. The consultant's placement in the communications structure needs to be reinforced by other forms of political access. The consultant may not just rely upon the presumed dependency which the mystique of his expertise can give him. He may actively seek support for the demand he is making. His ability to generate this support will be conditional on his possession, control and tactical ability in using three additional power resources. His assessed stature in the locus of power in his organization. The amount of political access he has and its corollary, his sensitivity and use of political information and processes. And finally, the amount and quality of group support he can mobilize from his peers. As we suggested earlier, the ability of an internal consultant to influence a client is a function of at least two interdependencies. That between consultant and consultant and that between consultant and client. Power is a systemic and not just a relational phenomenon.

POLITICAL ACCESS AND SENSITIVITY

To the internal consultant interested in the acceptance and implementation of his ideas, political access is likely to be critical. In the political processes which surround many organizational changes the ideas which remain supreme will not necessarily be a product of the greater worthiness or weight of issues ranged behind them, but rather in the nature of the linkages which opposing parties have to individuals over whom they are competing for support. (For detailed empirical examples of this in a study of computer purchase decisions, see Pettigrew[1973b].) The amount of support a consultant achieves is likely to be conditional on the structure and nature of his direct and indirect interpersonal reltionships.

The present discussion of political strategies is based on the assumption that men seek to adjust social conditions to achieve their ends. This view of man does not assume that all behaviour is self-interested. Neither is it assumed that the process of adjusting means to ends is a rational one. Individual choices are limited by their perception of the situation on which they base their strategies. As Kapferer (1969) notes, individuals continually commit errors because of misperception through lack of information or miscalculation. They may also be manoeuvred into commiting errors. A final and significant restriction on rationality is the constraints of access imposed by man's location in a network of social relations.

The politically aware consultant is likely to be conscious of the span of his social network, the degree of reciprocity in those contacts and the extent to which the relationship are uniplex or multiplex (Gluckman, 1956; Kapferer, 1969). All interactions are composed of a number of transactions or exchange contents. They might be conversation, personal service, job assistance and social related interactions. The latter in an organizational setting might be spending coffee or lunch periods together and a range of after-work social and sporting contact. Multiplexity refers to the number of exchange contents in any relationship. A relationship becomes multiplex when there is more than one exchange conent within it. A uniplex relationship has only one exchange content. The present theory of social power argues that multiplex relationships are 'stronger' than those which are uniplex. Generally speaking the consultant will be able to exert greater pull and influence over the client to whom he is multiplexly tied.

How focused the consultant's network is to the locus of power in the organization is also critical. Clearly there is little political advantage in having a network with an extensive span of multiplex relationships if they are with individuals with little power. The consultant should be sensitive to the relative power of those he endeavours to attract. Along with a reasoned perception must come effective action. Bailey (1969, p. 108) makes this point well.

'Knowledge is power. The man who correctly understands how a particular structure works can prevent it from working or make it work differently with much less effort than a man who does not know these things. This may seem obvious yet actions are often taken without previous analysis, and out of ignorance.'

ASSESSED STATURE

It should be clear from the preceding discussion that the mobilization and tactical use of power rests on the understanding of at least three general elements. A power aspirant with his set of potential power resources. Some mode of interpersonal activity or other communication, and a recipient of the influence attempt. The notion of assessed stature not only seems to be critical power resource for the internal consultant (Pettigrew, 1973b); it also serves as away of conceptually linking the above three elements of the power process.

Consultants do not merely advise, they persuade, negotiate and exercise the power they can mobilize. Assuming the consultant is both able to successfully identify and has access to the centre of power in his organization, an important constraint on his ability to negotiate and persuade is likely to be his assessed stature, both in that centre of power and in his immediate interpersonal relationships with clients. Assessed stature is defined as the process of developing positive feelings in the perceptions of relevant others.

The development of assessed stature may be linked to what Goffman (1969) has to say about impression management. 'When an individual enters the presence of others, he will want to discover the facts of the situation. Were he to possess this information, he could know, and make allowances for, what will come to happen and he could give the others present as much of their due as is consistent with his enlightened self-interest' (Goffman, 1969, p. 220). What is critical, yet imprecisely defined by Goffman here, are 'the facts of the situation'. From this author's viewpoint the process of accruing the facts of the situation may be conceptualized as identifying client role saliences.

Before discussing the meaning of role saliences it may be opportune to quote some examples of what occurs when role saliences are not exposed by a party making an influence attempt. Studies by Triandis (1960a, 1960b), on superior-subordinate relationships supported the general proposition that the greater the cognitive dissimilarity between two persons the less effective will be the communication between them and the less satisfied they will be with their relationship.

In a later study, this time of interpersonal relationships in international organizations, Triandis (1967) substantially upheld his hypothesis that work associates who belong to different cultures will experience severe communication problems and low levels of affect towards each other. A less precisely researched but more poignant example of the failure to anticipate role saliences in others is offered by Hall (1968, pp. 10-11). He describes a series of unproductive meetings between American and Greek diplomats where the assumptions and behaviour patterns of each side were misunderstood and the result was a slow but inevitable break-up of the exchanges.

Clearly what is established from the Triandis (1967) study and Hall's example of interpersonal misunderstandings in diplomatic negotiations, is that if parties to such relationships are to influence one another they must be in the position to identify what is salient in the other party's perspective and behaviour. The concept of role salience recognizes that different groups of clients and consultants have varying sets of needs, expectations and reference group affiliations. They also relate to others with differing sets of political interests. The present suggestion is that a consultant's ability to anticipate what is salient for the client in these terms is an important component of the process of generating a high assessed stature for himself. Clearly the assessment and anticipation of these saliences will be that much easier for a consultant with a social network with an extensive span and with multiplex rather than uniplex relationships across that network.

Clark (1974) argues that exchange theory can be used to aid this process of anticipation. He suggests monitoring the course of a project by mapping out power relations, role expectations and pay-off matrices of the various actors in the consultant-client system and intervening to control sources of variance.

In this discussion, the concept of assessed stature is not equivalent to the French and Raven (1966) notion of referent power. The consultant is not trying to 'identify' or develop a 'feeling of oneness' with the client. Rather the consultant is seeking to identify and thereby anticipate what is salient for the client both in task and political terms, so that his proposals may be formulated to receive minimal client resistance and maximal support from the locus of power in his organization.

In the early stages of any client-consultant relationship part of the tactics of generating high assesed stature may involve demonstrating competence in areas salient to the client. This has been described by some consultants as 'the low key approach'. The consultant takes on small jobs perceived to be salient for client needs and whose successful outcome can be priced in pounds sterling. This way the consultant builds up credits for himself with significant others and later is able to generate support for projects whose salience to others is not so readily discernible.

Alongside the consultant's ability to generate high assessed stature must come the ability to perceive when he has high and low stature. Power derived from stature is a variable phenomenon. Political timing, therefore, becomes important. The time and the way a proposal is presented may have a crucial impact on the support it receives. The consultant seeking to mobilize power must be careful to make his assertions at a time when he has the resources to enforce his will. The consultant with low stature does not make demands on the system that threatens him. See Pettigrew (1973b) for a case example of how the Head of Management Services in a company timed his political demands in a competitive decision-making situation to match the points when his stature with the client system peaked.

GROUP SUPPORT

Arguments in previous sections have indicated that expertise, control over information, and political access and sensitivity are necessary but not sufficient conditions for consultant power. The possession and tactical use of these power resources needs to be considered in the context of the consultant's assessed stature in the social arena he works.

There is at least one other important variable feeding into this system, the amount and kind of group support given to the internal consultant by his colleagues in his own department and in related consultant groups. A major constraint on political activity in all organizations is the amount of time and energy so consumed. In this writer's research experience (Pettigrew, 1973a, 1973b), protracted power struggles between internal consultant groups use up a great deal of the reserves of time and energy these groups might have more profitably used assisting one another in generating support for their ideas with client groups.

The co-ordination problems posed by internal consultant groups such as operations researchers, systems analysts, programmers and financial planners relate particularly to their emergent status (Pettigrew, 1973a). The task environment shared by developing specialities is often poorly institutionalized. That is to say, the system of role relationships, norms and sanctions which regulate access to different positions and sets of activities lacks both clarity and consistency. In the absence of such clarity and consistency a process of role crystallization takes place. Eisenstadt (1965, p. 31). Strauss et al. (1964) have described the strategic aspects of this crystallization as the negotiation of order.

Problems of status and power arise as the emergent consultant groups seek social accreditation. Some groups take on expansionist policies, intrude on others' domains and provoke conflict. The process of the conflict between the rival groups may take on the form of a set of boundary testing activities. As one group seeks power and the other survival, each will develop a set of stereotypes and misconceptions about each other. A group declining in status and power may seek to emphasize that part of the core of its expertise which still remains and which may not be covered by the activities of the expanding group. This may be interpreted as a threat by the newer group who are likely to be defensive about their own history of inexpertise in this area. They in turn may retaliate by emphasizing their particular strength. In this way one group's defensive behaviour becomes another group's threat and the cycle of conflict continues.

The *resolution* of such structural conflicts seems questionable. The conflicts have been *regulated*, however, through a variety of integrative mechanisms. These include creating integrative roles, project teams, project controllers and training in interpersonal skills (Lawrence & Lorsch, 1967; Baker & Schaffer, 1969; Walton, 1969).

However, an additional problem remains. Apparently, some client groups are prepared to encourage conflict between and amongst consultant groups as a way of controlling them more effectively. Wilensky (1967, p. 51) argues Roosevelt's technique for controlling his technical subordinates was to 'keep grants of authority incomplete, jurisdictions uncertain, charters overlapping'. Pettigrew (1973b, p. 145) quote the example of a Board of Directors' use of this approach.

'By keeping distant from the scene of conflict, by giving the programmers some freedom from the system of bureaucratic rules, and by keeping job assignments uncertain, subject to change at any moment, they prevented the programmers from consolidating in a stable power base, and still managed to extract the knowledge and work necessary for the company's continued prosperity.'

Power conflicts between internal consultant groups are likely to be a continuing feature of organizational life. Issues concerned with the relative share of interdependent activities and the distribution of status and power are only fundamentally defused when the groups are either no longer interdependent or the supremacy of one group becomes so clear that further protest from the other is perceived to be futile. In the continuing absence of either of these conditions, the political position of consultant group vis-à-vis client groups will be that much the weaker.

CONCLUSION

This paper has sought to emphasize the essentially political character of organizational life. Internal consultant-client relationships take place in the context of organizations where struggles for the advancement and maintenance of power and status are pervasive and real. The origins and momentum for these political processes are in part the continual changes that most organizations experience. Major structural changes have political consequences.

Internal consultants have a vested interest in change. This is how they legitimate their presence. Many client groups have a vested interest in relative stability. They have quotas to reach, deadlines to meet and empires to protect. There is no reason to expect them to readily accept changes which are against their interests. That is why the relationship between internal consultants and clients is regarded as a problem one.

The present concern has been to conceptualize the mobilization of consultant power. Power was defined as a causal relation between the preferences of an actor regarding an outcome and the outcome itself. Power involves the ability of a consultant to produce outcomes consonant with his perceived interests. The base of the consultant's power rests on his possession, control and tactical use of five resources. These were expertise, control of information, political access and sensitivity, assessed stature and peer and related consultant group support. Of these the first three appear to be necessary but not sufficient conditions for consultant power. Once he has the political access and understanding, the consultant's ability to negotiate and persuade depends on his assessed stature with the appropriate figures in his political network.

Part of the process of generating high assessed stature rests on the consultant's ability to manage the impressions he creates with others. Given the relatively high levels of stress in the consultant's role and what we know about cognitive and perceptual impairment under stress, this process of impression management is not an easy one. Generating and maintaining stature during a project appears to be associated with the consultant's ability to identify and thereby anticipate role saliences of clients and or key figures in his political network. These role saliences refer not only to the client's values, expectancies and reference groups but also to his political and career interests and how they might be affected by any consultant proposals. Credit can be built up by attending to projects which relate particularly to client saliencies. This is especially so if the benefits of the project can be expressed unequivocally in financial terms. These credits may then be 'cashed' on projects the consultant has a particular interest in.

Finally, this analysis has highlighted the significance to the consultant of his ability to form multiplex relationships with key figures in his political network. On the development of these relationships depends the consultant's capacity to identify role saliencies in others and also to assess clearly and accurately when his stature is high and low. It would seem to be important for the consultant to time his influence attempts to coincide with periods when his assessed stature is high. It is suggested that further research using the above concepts will not only help in the analysis of internal consultant-client relationships but also in the development of a political theory of intervention in organizations.

REFERENCES

Argyris, C. *Intervention theory and method: A behavioural science view.* Reading, MA: Addison-Wesley, 1970.
Bailey, F. G. *Stratagems and spoils: A social anthropology of politics.* Oxford: Basil Blackwell, 1969. ·

Baker, J. K., & Schaffer, R. H. Making staff consulting more effective. *Harvard Business Review*, 1969, 63-71.

Bannester, D. M. Socio-dynamics: An integrating theorem of power, authority, interinfluence and love. *American Sociological Review*, 1969, 24, 374-393.

Bennis, W. *Organization development: Its nature, origins and prospects.* Reading, MA: Addison-Wesley, 1969.

Blau, P. M. *Exchange and power in social life.* New York: John Wiley, 1964.

Burns, T. & Stalker, G. M. *The management of innovation.* London: Tavistock, 1961.

Clark, A. W. The client-practitioner relationship as an inter-system engagement. In A. W. Clark (Ed.) *Experience in action research.* London: Malaby, 1974.

Crozier, M. *The bureaucratic phenomenon.* London: Tavistock, 1964.

Dalton, M. *Men who manage.* New York: John Wiley, 1959.

Eisenstadt, S. N. *Essays in comparative institutions.* New York: John Wiley, 1965.

Emerson, R. M. Power-dependence relations. *American Sociological Review*, 1962, 27, 33-41.

French, J.R.P., & Raven, B. The bases of social power. In D. Cartwright (Ed.), *Studies in social power* (2nd ed.). Ann Arbor, MI: Institute for Social Research.

Gluckman, M. *Custom and conflict in Africa.* Oxford: Basil Blackwell, 1956.

Goffman, I. *The presentation of self in everyday life.* London: Penguin Press, 1969.

Hall, E. T. *The silent language.* New York: Fawcett, 1968.

Hickson, D. J., Hinings, C. R., Lee, C. A., Schneck, R. E., & Jennings, N. M. A strategic contingencies theory of intraorganisational power. *Administrative Science Quarterly*, 1971, 16 (2), 216-229.

Jaques, E. *The changing culture of a factory.* London: Tavistock, 1951.

Kahn, R. L., Wolfe, D. M., Snoek, R. P., Diedrick, J., & Rosenthal, R. A. *Organizational stress.* New York: John Wiley, 1964.

Kapferer, B. *Urban Africans at work.* Unpublished Ph.D. thesis, University of Manchester, Dept. of Social Anthropology, 1969.

Kotler, P. The elements of social action. In Gerald Zaltman, Philip Kotler, & Ira Kaufman (Eds.), *Creating social change.* New York: Holt, Rinehart & Winston, 1972.

Lawrence, P. R. & Lorsch, J. W. *Organisation and environment.* Cambridge, MA: Harvard University Press, 1967.

McCleery, R. Communication patterns as bases of systems of authority and power. *Theoretical studies in social organisation of the prison.* New York: S.S.R.C. Pamphlet, March 15, 1960.

March, J. G., & Simon, H. A. *Organisation.* New York: John Wiley, 1958.

Mechanic, D. Sources of power of lower participants in complex organisations. *Administrative Science Quarterly*, 1962, 7(3), 349-364.

Pettigrew, A. M. Inter-group conflict and role strain. *Journal of Management Studies*, 1968, 5(2), 205-218.

Pettigrew, A. M. Information control as a power resource, *Sociology*, 1972, 6(2), 187-204.

Pettigrew, A. M. Occupational specialisation as an emergent process. *Sociological Review*, 1973, 21(2), 255-278.(a)

Pettigrew, A. M. *The politics of organizational decision-making.* London: Tavistock, 1973.(b).

Rhenman, E. *Organization theory for long-range planning.* London: John Wiley, 1973.

Strauss, A., Schatzman, L., Bucher, R., Ehrlich, D., & Sabshin, M. *Psychiatric ideologies and institutions.* New York: Free Press, 1964.

Triandis, H. C. Cognitive similarity and communication in a dyad. *Human Relations,* 1960, 13, 175-183. (a)

Triandis, H. C. Some determinants of interpersonal communication. *Human Relations,* 1960, 13, 279-287. (b)

Triandis, H. C. Interpersonal relations in international organizations. *Organisational Behaviour and Human Performance,* 1967, 2, 26-55.

Walton, R. E. Two strategies of social change and their dilemmas. *Journal of Applied Behavioral Science,* 1965, 2, 167-179.

Walton, R. E. *Interpersonal peacemaking: Confrontation and third party consultation.* Reading, MA: Addison-Wesley, 1969.

Whyte, W. F. & Hamilton, E. L. *Action research for management.* Homewood, IL: Irwin Dorsey, 1964.

Wilensky, H. L. *Organisational intelligence.* New York: Basic Books, 1967.

Zaltman, G. Strategies for social change. In Gerald Zaltman, Philip Kotler, & Ira Kaufman (Eds.), *Creating social change.* New York: Holt, Rinehart & Winston, 1972.

4

Research and Implementation
A Case Study

☐ Research with implementation in mind requires a very different outlook on the part of the researcher than does research that does not have action objectives. The researcher must be concerned about the motivation of the client or research subjects to provide valid data and to act on the conclusions of the research. Assessing client motivation to change and/or developing it through involving employees and managers therefore becomes very important. Involvement must be fostered in planning the research, interpreting findings, and planning action. Similarly, the perceived relevance of the research questions and instruments is as important as the scientific rigor (by "normal science" standards) of the research design and method. While client motivation and involvement and scientific rigor are not mutually exclusive, in many instances rigor can be obtained only at a cost to involvement. This is because traditional scientific methods typically call for more distance between the researcher and the client and more control over the research process by the researcher than by the client. The conflict between rigor and client motivation represents a major dilemma to be managed by the researcher whose goal is research and implementation.

There are conceptual frameworks and ideas that can be very helpful to researchers seeking implementation of research findings. Ideas about entry, contracting, diagnosis, data collection, data feedback, and problem solving that are associated with organization development, action research, and intervention theory and methods are relevant to the problems of research with implementation in mind (see the reference list at the end of the book). Effectiveness in managing research with implementation in mind requires skills in diagnosing one's own motivation as a researcher, the client's motivation, and skills in making a number of strategic and tactical choices in planning and implementing the research. These choices are situationally determined. Therefore the researcher must analyze the client's state of readiness to act on findings and make tactical decisions about the research process. The case that follows raises issues about research methodology and researcher values, tactical skills, and thought processes needed to conduct research with implementation in mind. Since the case involves a research project intended to result in the implementation of a stress reduction program, an article by Ivancevich and Matteson (1980) should be read to give you a perspective on job stress from which you should "second guess" the researcher and managers portrayed in the case. The case describes an effort to do research with implementation in mind and thus allows a critique of the strategy and tactics employed by the researcher. The Ivancevich and Matteson article provides background about the content area being researched and should be read so that you can evaluate the researchers' efforts, and, after discussion of the issues, develop alternative research strategies that might increase the probability of relieving job stress while contributing to knowledge.

If you have never participated in a case discussion we suggest the following steps for preparation. Read the case quickly to get a sense of the whole. Then read the article. Following your reading of the article, look at the questions provided below as a guide to developing a deeper analysis of the case. Go back to the case and dig out the facts, events, motivations, interchanges, and other causal variables that help explain what happened. Think about what alternatives were available to the researcher. Make some notes to yourself. Be ready to discuss what happened at Comp Graf.

CASE PREPARATION QUESTIONS

(1) What has prevented the implementation of George Simon's research findings at Comp Graf? Analyze factors in the company, the research design, the process of planning and communicating with management, and forces within Simon himself.

(2) What were key choice points in the process at which a different approach by Simon might have changed the outcome? What signals did Simon get to indicate that he had problems? Be prepared to list these and suggest how you might have approached things differently.

(3) What should Simon do now? Prepare an action plan and provide a rationale for it.

(4) If your objective were to implement research findings on stress at Comp Graf, how would you have gone about designing and implementing the research? Develop an alternative research design and an implementation plan.

COMP GRAF, INC.: A CASE OF RESEARCH WITH IMPLEMENTATION IN MIND

It was the first day of the new year and Dr. George Simon, an industrial/organizational (I/O) psychologist and researcher in the area of preventive health and stress management sat back to reflect on his accomplishments during the previous year. Despite the festive atmosphere of the holiday season, he had not been able to relax and enjoy himself. He could not convince himself that he had accomplished what he had set out to do during 1980.

Simon had hoped that by January 1, 1981, he would have achieved two major goals. First, he had hoped to complete a major research project on the organizational correlates of stress among managers and professionals in industry. This was a research program on which he had been working for three years that spanned several medium- to large-sized companies. Second, and much more importantly to him in 1980, he had hoped that a research project at Comp Graf, Inc., would not only add more data to his already large bank, but would end in implementation of an action program to reduce stress in that organization. By collecting pretest and posttest data, Simon was hoping to document changes stemming from the program. These he hoped to publish in a refereed journal as a capstone to his present program. But, he was also eager to see his research efforts pay off in successful implementation.

Now, more than eleven months after Fred McMulty, President of Comp Graf, Inc., had agreed to sponsor his research project, there was little to show for his efforts. To be sure, he had collected valuable data on more than 500 of Comp Graf's managers and professionals, but little had been accomplished in the implementation of his findings. After hundreds of questionnaires, a significant amount of time and money in analysis of this data, and many meetings with managers in the company, Comp Graf was not implementing a systematic program to reduce stress. While some managers had asked him to recommend ways in which the research data might be used, this level of interest hardly justified the effort.

Beyond the lack of success in implementation, two problems worried Simon. He had received a call from McMulty a week earlier during which the president had expressed disappointment that there was little to show for such a substantial investment of money and time. As McMulty told him:

Very little is happening to reduce stress around here. Just yesterday one of my most brilliant engineers left saying he couldn't take this place anymore. He told me his ulcer is acting up, his family is upset, and that he can't get anything done in this place. Frankly, George, your research project had created *more* stress around here. I am feeling it even more than I was before we started the project.

Even more worrying were Simon's growing questions about the whole research project. The experience at Comp Graf had reduced his faith in the data he had accumulated and placed into the computer. He had learned so many new things as a result of his interactions with managers that he wondered what all that data really meant and how useful it would be in implementing a stress management program.

GEORGE SIMON AND HIS RESEARCH

In 1975, George Simon received his Ph.D. in industrial/organizational psychology at the age of 28, from a large mid-western university. His training had included many of the traditional content areas included in an I/O program ranging from selection and training topics to organizational psychology. In addition, he had received substantial training in research methodology. This included training in research design, field research methods, and multivariate statistics. From the beginning, he had been interested in the problem of stress, and his Ph.D. thesis was in this area.

The stress research program that he had been conducting in the last three years had its roots in his Ph.D. research. Based on this initial small-scale study and survey of the literature, he became convinced that stress among managers and professionals could be explained in part by characteristics of the job such as quantitative overload (too much work for the time and energy level of the individual), qualitative overload (work that is too challenging given the capacity of the individual), unexplained and frequent changes in direction, too little control over one's work, too little feedback of results, and so on. Most previous research and writing had been concerned with relating psychological and physiological symptoms of stress (i.e., blood pressure, high cholesterol, anxiety, fatigue, and poor decision making) to personality characteristics such as low tolerance of ambiguity, low flexibility, and Type A behavior patterns. Simon felt that this research overlooked the importance of factors inherent in the job itself that might be causing Type A patterns of behavior and stress. If this were true, a program of stress management would have to change those job characteristics most related to stress. In Simon's view, stress management programs such as biofeedback, exercise, progressive relaxation, meditation, and others had been aimed exclusively at relieving the symptoms of stress, not at eliminating the causes of the stress. Simon became interested in studying the relationship between job factors and psychological, physiological, and organizational variables such as absenteeism, satisfaction, and productivity. Understanding these relationships, he felt, would lead to a stress management program that would go to the root of the stress.

The research design included a long questionnaire that tapped a number of relevant job factors, as well as attitudes such as feelings of stress, job satisfaction, anxiety, and self-report about behavioral patterns. Corporate data on turnover, absenteeism, performance, and physiological information from yearly medical exams were also to be included as criterion variables. The questionnaire also included some personality measures that were assumed to be moderators of the relationship between job factors and stress symptoms. Multivariate statistical techniques over time were to be the primary means of analysis.

Over a three-year period, four companies had been approached to cooperate and this research was in progress. Comp Graf was approached in early 1980 and was selected as the fifth research site, but the only site in which Simon hoped implementation of a "stress control" program would result. In all five research sites the cost of the research was to be paid by the organization.

Simon's objective was to complete the program of research by mid-1981 and to publish results in a series of articles and a book.

COMP GRAF, INC.

THE BUSINESS

Comp Graf, Inc., is an organization involved in the design, development, manufacturing, and marketing of process-control monitoring systems; such systems provide real-time visual feedback of process-type manufacturing operations. Comp Graf pioneered the use of color graphics displays in process monitoring. Their minicomputer-based systems replaced older dial and strip-chart recorder monitoring methods. It was widely acknowledged in industry circles that Comp Graf's rapid growth and success were due to its innovative and superior product technology.

Process-control monitoring systems are used in a number of different industries. Comp Graf has directed its marketing and sales efforts toward large companies in the chemical processing, food processing, and utility plant industries. A Comp Graf system sells for approximately $300,000. Sales in 1980 were $100 million, and profits were $5 million. Like most rapidly growing, high-technology companies, Comp Graf required large amounts of capital to finance its growth. These came from profits, loans, and venture capital. The requirement for cash and capital put continual pressure on top management to meet forecasted profits.

Comp Graf had 31 percent share of the current graphics processing market. Its five major competitors had 37 percent, 14 percent, 9 percent, and 6 percent of market share, respectively. As mentioned previously, the graphic system industry is characterized by a rapid rate of technological advancement. As a result, the industry is highly competitive. To continue to grow, gain market share, or simply maintain its position in the marketplace, Comp Graf must actively market its product to generate sales. Active marketing is also important to build up orders backlog. The organization aims for a steady 25 million backlog of orders. In addition, an organization in the process control industry must constantly develop more efficient, more advanced, and less expensive products. According to one manager,

> This is a highly pressurized and competitive industry. To survive you have to be one step ahead of everyone else. Every six months there is a significant change in one market place. That kind of activity puts a lot of pressure on everyone, engineering, particularly sales and marketing. People simply don't wait in line to buy a $300,000 computer.

THE HISTORY OF THE COMPANY

Comp Graf began in 1965 when Fred McMulty, a Ph.D. in electrical engineering, and three of his associates from Lincoln Laboratories at MIT, decided to go into business for themselves. McMulty became president and the others became officers of the company. Headquarters were set up in McMulty's living room. Comp Graf's engineers worked together closely that first year and in 1970 introduced the first color graphic process-monitoring systems ever to appear on the market. The systems were well received, particularly in the food-processing industry, and by 1972 Comp Graf was growing at the rate of 50 percent per year. In 1980 Comp Graf was a very different organization than it had been initially. McMulty and one of his colleagues, Jim Ardmore, were still involved in company management. The other two had left to go back to Lincoln Laboratories, where they continued their research and development interests. As Comp Graf grew, it relocated and finally was housed north of Boston in six separate buildings within 15 minutes of each other. In January 1980 when Simon first approached the company, it employed some 2000 people, of which 500 were salaried and professional.

Despite the rapid growth and profitability, the company was not without problems. In an industry in which the average turn-over rate is from 12 to 15 percent, Comp Graf experienced a 30 percent rate in 1977, a 25 percent rate in 1978, and still a 20 percent rate in 1979. Although the top management team was stable—except for the resignation of two of the original founders— engineers, programmers, technicians, and marketing people would come and go quickly. Comp Graf's business is characterized by high and ever-changing technology. Employee loss can be a serious problem in that type of situation, because qualified people are in high demand but in extremely short supply. The process of recruiting, interviewing, and hiring costs the company both time and money.

BUSINESS STATUS

Since 1965 net sales at Comp Graf had grown at a compound rate of about 50 percent per year. In early 1980, when George Simon first became involved with Comp Graf, 1979 results were in. Actual total revenues were less than had been predicted. Income before taxes, however, was about the same as predicted for 1979. Nevertheless, concern was building about the financial situation. Simon recalled a conversation with Mark Thomas, vice president of finance, in January 1980, shortly after he had become involved with Comp Graf:

> In August of 1979 we had just finished a big half. By December, though, we were behind our predictions. We hadn't thought the usual fall doldrums would affect business that year, but apparently they did. We had to readjust our thinking and cut down our forecasts for 1980. We had originally predicted a $140 million year in 1980 but we had to readjust that to $125 million.

Comp Graf managers were also concerned with company finances. According to a manager in the manufacturing department, who also talked with Simon in January 1980:

> We all know in an industry like this we need a backlog. By the end of last year (1979) we had really eaten away and were continuing to eat away at the order backlog we had. At that point our backlog was only 15 million and from what I understand, we just aren't getting orders.

THE ORGANIZATION AND CULTURE

Of Comp Graf's 2000 employees, 75 were executives and managerial staff. The president and vice president of finance were housed in one of the six buildings, while engineering, marketing, manufacturing, and customer service each occupied their own separate building. All but one of the buildings were within walking distance.

Comp Graf is headed by Fred McMulty, who is responsible to a 12-member board of directors of which he and the other vice presidents were members. Reporting to McMulty are five functions—marketing, manufacturing, engineering, finance, and customer service. All but the customer service function are headed by vice presidents (see Figures 4.1 and 4.2 for organization chart and background of executives). The marketing function is headed by Bob Jones, who has reporting to him a domestic sales manager, four product managers, and a marketing and sales manager in charge of international business. The product managers are responsible for profitability and are considered business managers and entrepreneurs for their business. Since they do not have sales, manufacturing, engineering, or finance reporting to them, they have to obtain the cooperation of managers in other functions to implement their business plans. Coordination between these functions is important because changing market conditions have to be continually reflected in changed engineering, manufacturing, and sales programs.

Over the past 15 years, Comp Graf had developed its own distinctive set of values and modus operandi. These reflected the beliefs of Fred McMulty. As described in a company handbook, Comp Graf culture is:

> a catch-all phrase attempting to describe notions peculiar to the company. Words or expressions associated with "Comp Graf Culture" can be:
>
> —unstructured.   —informal.
>
> —make it happen.   —rapid growth.

Board of Directors

President
Fred McMulty

Manager Customer Service Sam Templeton	V.P. Finance Mark Thomas	V.P. Manufacturing Dave Bertram	V. P. Engineering Jim Ardmore	V. P. Marketing Bob Jones
R. Kennedy National Tech. Supplies Manager	C. Lavin Contracts Manager	C. Peters Quality Control Manager	N. Eanen Engineering Manager Food Processing	D. Crosby Marketing Manager
P. Eckke National Operating Manager	D. Gray Data Processing Manager	D. Patterson Peripheral Products	P. Richmond Engineering Manager Utilities	B. Ellis National Sales Manager
D. Fahr Materials Manager	M. Peatrenk Controller	R. Gibley Materials Manager	L. Cires Engineering Manager Chemical Industries	Product Managers International Sales Manager (open)
S. Wright Software Supplies Manager	P. O'Connell Assistant Treasurer	S. Shiba Manufacturing Engineering & Shop Operations Manager	Engineering Manager New Product Development (unfilled)	
	R. Long Personnel			
M. Mitchell France				
P. Bernheimer Germany				
T. Daily England				

Figure 4.1   Comp Graf, Inc.: Organization Chart

—a positive approach   —controlled chaos.
   toward people.

Hallmarks of Comp Graf culture are ambiguity, freedom, flexibility, risk taking, and a supportive attitude toward employees.

Jim Ardmore, vice president of engineering, wrote in a memo to incoming employees:

You must be a self-starter and self-director. Only you can really decide what is the right thing to do. If you really believe in doing something, do it, even if you are told no. Be prepared to get killed if you are wrong. Tell the right people what you are going to do even

Fred McMulty: President, 40 years old. Dr. McMulty received a B.S., M.S., and Ph.D. in Engineering from Berkeley. During his graduate studies, Dr. McMulty consulted for several organizations in the area of process control. After a brief period as a professor at Berkeley, he went to work in research at Lincoln Labs at MIT. He worked there for two years and founded Comp Graf in 1969. Dr. McMulty is a member of Comp Graf's Board of Directors.

Bob Jones: Vice President, Marketing, 42 years old. Mr. Jones received an undergraduate degree from Fordham and an MBA from New York University. After his graduate education he went to work for Exxon, then Pitney Bowes in sales. He was recruited by a search firm and came to Comp Graf in 1966. Jones is also a member of Comp Graf's Board of Directors.

Jim Ardmore: Vice President, Engineering, 43 years old. Ardmore received a B.S. in Engineering at the University of Arkansas. He continued his education in engineering at the University of Illinois and received a Ph.D. After finishing his doctorate Ardmore went to work at MIT, stayed there for one year, and left to begin Comp Graf in 1965. He is a member of Comp Graf's Board of Directors.

Dave Bertram: Vice President, Manufacturing, 38 years old. Mr. Bertram received a B.S. in Engineering at the University of Rhode Island. He continued his education at Wharton and earned an MBA. After graduate school Mr. Bertram went to work for General Electric in manufacturing, where he worked for 6 years, before being recruited and joining Comp Graf in 1973. Mr. Bertram is also a member of the Board of Directors.

Mark Thomas: Vice President, Finance, 39 years old. Mark earned a B.S. in Electrical Engineering from Case Western Reserve and an MBA from Harvard. He went to work for IBM directly out of Harvard, in finance and pricing. He stayed with IBM for several years before joining and working with an investment banking firm for one year. His next job involved venture capital work at General Electric. While at GE he invested GE's and his own money in Comp Graf. He became a member of the Board of Directors in 1975, and left GE to join Comp Graf.

Sam Templeton: Manager, Customer Service, 34 years old. He earned a B.A. from St. Anselms College, went to work in the Peace Corps, and then spent eight years as a manager at the United Parcel Service Company. He and McMulty were neighbors and friends. He was personally recruited to Comp Graf by McMulty.

Figure 4.2   Comp Graf, Inc.: Personnel Profiles

if you say you disagree. . . . Get accustomed to radical changes in organization and jobs people are doing, including your own. Be prepared for surprising and unpredictable changes every couple of years.

President Fred McMulty once explained how to succeed at Comp Graf:

> There are no rules. Do a good job. It may take a while before people appreciate and notice what you're doing, but in the long run it's the job that counts. . . . . Sometimes we move people so fast that they don't gain any experience because we are constantly short of good people. Ideally you should really stay in an area long enough to live with your mistakes. The biggest thing to learn is the results of your mistakes.

In line with many tenets of the Comp Graf culture, the company had not placed great emphasis on planning. While not all agreed, it was not uncommon for people to express little faith in planning. As one manager put it, "The planning process doesn't drive anything." In light of the company's remarkable history, it was not unusual for Comp Graf's old-timers to feel that if things had worked out before without much long-range planning, they would do so again.

Fred McMulty characterized himself as an entrepreneur and fire fighter. He said of the company, "We've trained, hired, and rewarded entrepreneurs and firemen around here." Primarily, McMulty dealt with managers in one-to-one meetings, often unplanned. He would drop into their office to talk about one problem or another. He met with his staff as a group twice a month. Typically, McMulty ran the meeting. He'd go around the room and ask for informal updates on what was happening. There was rarely any discussion of issues that were raised; the meeting was primarily for information sharing. On occasion he would present an idea on some kind of corporate plan or organizational idea and ask for input, which he would use to make decisions. Simon recalled that in his first meeting, McMulty described his management style as follows:

> I generally make most of the organizational decisions around here. When we first started the company I did everything. I made all the

decisions and didn't really explain to anybody why I made them. I was in a position, though, to have a very complete picture of the organization, and was the only one in a position to make good decisions. As the organization has grown I have tried to change my style. I let certain people make decisions, but I don't feel that right now I can delegate all or even most of the decision making. I tend to be a bit of a perfectionist and expect an awful lot. I feel as though I am ahead of the organization in terms of knowing or thinking about where we are going, where we ought to be, and what ought to be done. I have a tendency to figure things out on my own, make assumptions, and make decisions. That confuses people sometimes, but I think it's what we need right now. I use the information I'm given at executive meetings but really make final decisions mostly myself.

Following the bimonthly staff meetings, each vice president met with his own department manager to communicate organizational plans and decisions or discuss company or department activities. Such meetings were the only source of information and direction for key managers in each function.

GETTING STARTED WITH RESEARCH
AT COMP GRAF

George Simon's initial contact with Comp Graf came through meeting Rick Long, personnel manager at Comp Graf, at a seminar on stress that he conducted during the summer of 1979 at the university. Simon remembered that Long was very interested in the seminar and felt that many of the stress symptoms and causes discussed in the seminar applied to Comp Graf. When Simon cited work overload and jobs that demand more competence than their incumbents possess as important causes of stress, Long said:

That's us. People in our company are constantly overloaded and have all those symptoms. I have heard that when people are brought into the emergency room of Emerson Hospital those on duty immediately say that it must be another Comp Graf manager.

Long attended the seminars because he had felt for some time that turnover, morale problems, people feeling overworked, high divorce rate, and health problems were due to the high levels of stress that people experienced at Comp Graf. Simon remembered that according to Long, managers at Comp Graf, including McMulty and most of his staff, agreed that stress was a major problem.

Simon told Long about his research and expressed an interest in Comp Graf as a possible research site. Simon and Long discussed that possibility at the seminar, and on the telephone later. They finally agreed that Simon would visit the company to discuss his research and determine whether there was interest in it. Long told him in a phone conversation just before coming that Bob Jones, the marketing manager, was feeling a lot of distress and would be a definite supporter of the research. Simon was excited! Comp Graf constituted a unique opportunity. It was a high technology company unlike others in his sample, and would allow interesting cross-company comparisons. It might also be a site in which he could get some interest in completing his research findings. He had been looking for a site just like it for over a year.

THE INITIAL VISIT

The first visit to Comp Graf was made in early November 1979. He met Long at his office. As he walked in the door of Comp Graf he expected to find a carpeted office with a receptionist and an expensive waiting room. Instead there were no carpets or easy chairs, just a metal desk and chairs. People were dressed in everything from coat and ties to jeans. Most people did not wear ties and seemed to be applying themselves to their work with great energy.

During his initial visit with Long, Simon outlined his research. He emphasized the following points about the research proposal.

(1) It would contribute to knowledge and understanding of stress and its causes.

(2) Good research in this area would ultimately lead to better theory.

(3) Comp Graf would obtain data about levels of stress and their relationship to job factors such as work overload. Data from other studies would provide normative data for comparison.

(4) Data on Comp Graf would be helpful to the company in implementing a program to reduce stress.

Later in the morning Long introduced Simon to Jones, the marketing manager. After presenting his ideas about the relationship between job factors and stress, Jones immediately jumped into the conversation with great enthusiasm and energy. He said:

You are right about overload and stress. Around here we are all overloaded and it's taking its toll. We make poor decisions, we never go home, and we crab at each other all the time. We in marketing seem to get the worst of it. Everyone is always pointing fingers at us and saying that we are the cause of problems around here. You know, maybe your research would help others see that it's not us but the way in which Fred runs this place. There is no planning, everything is at the last minute, and we have people who can't do the job they have. That's why there is so much stress.

Simon recalls feeling somewhat uneasy as Jones spoke, but his enthusiasm for the research project buoyed him. He left Jones's office certain that Jones would be a supporter of his research.

Simon left Comp Graf enthused. He had agreed to write a formal proposal for the research, which Long would send to McMulty. If the proposal were to catch McMulty's interest, Simon would come back to visit with him and make the sales pitch for the research at that level.

THE MEETING WITH McMULTY

After several unsuccessful attempts to set up a meeting with McMulty, Long finally succeeded in arranging a meeting in early

December. Simon recalled walking into McMulty's office and being surprised to find it small, furnished with a metal desk and process-control computer terminal. During their 40-minute meeting there were several phone calls and three or four personal interruptions. Simon presented the same points he had made to Long in the formal proposal. He stressed the value of the research to the field of industrial organizational psychology and to the firm. He emphasized that data from the study would be useful to the company in finding out how much stress there was and how job factors might be contributing to it. He described briefly the questionnaire approach and other physiological data he hoped to get with the cooperation of the medical department. He outlined the time and money ($5,000 to $6,000) it would take to complete the study.

McMulty, through distracted by interruptions, expressed interest in the study. He said that he himself was continually under a lot of pressure. He described a recent conversation with another corporate president that highlighted the problem for him.

> I was having lunch with an acquaintance of mine who is the president of a company that is about twice our current size. His firm has been growing at between 5 and 7 percent per year for the last 10 years. I was telling him about some of the decisions I had made during the previous two weeks and some of the decisions I had to make in the upcoming week. At one point he stopped me and said something like, "You know, you make as many important business decisions in a month as I do in a year." And while he may be exaggerating a bit, I think he is basically right. Since we grow at about 5 percent a month, I end up making decisions in a month that he gets nearly a year to make.

McMulty then said that at age 40, after fifteen years of building a company, the pressure was taking a toll on him and his family. He described how his wife kept reminding him about how little time he was spending with his children and that soon they would be gone. He then said:

> Lots of people around here are on edge. The stress sometimes shows in their work, and in their marriages. The divorce rate in our management group is considerably above the national average. We sure ought to do something about that and if your study can help, we ought to support it.

Simon left the meeting elated. McMulty had not only agreed to support the study, but seemed to have a personal interest in it. He had agreed to go ahead with the study and suggested that Simon make a presentation to his staff at their next bimonthly meeting at the end of December. With McMulty's personal interest in the study, implementation of findings seemed to Simon to be assured. McMulty said, "You know, Bob Jones was really enthusiastic about your research project and thinks it would help his group. He will be a big supporter."

THE MEETING WITH McMULTY AND HIS STAFF

In late December 1979, Simon and his research assistant met with McMulty and his staff. At the meeting were McMulty, his staff, Long, the personnel manager, and to Simon's surprise, several other managers who reported to McMulty's immediate subordinates. Several of these were product managers who reported to Jones, the marketing manager. Jones greeted Simon warmly and made a few remarks to others before the meeting had started that he had already talked with Simon and thought the research on stress was really needed. Several of the other managers who Simon did not know seemed ill at ease at this moment.

The plan for the meeting had been for Long, the personnel manager, to open the meeting and provide background. Simon and his research assistant were then to make their presentation about the research. Long and Simon had wanted McMulty to introduce Simon but he had declined, feeling that it was better for Long, who would coordinate the study, to kick things off. Besides, McMulty had said, "I don't want my staff to feel under any pressure to go along with the study." McMulty encouraged Long to get Jones to speak up for the study.

The meeting started at 3 p.m. After a brief introduction by Long, Simon began by encouraging the group to ask questions at any time. He then started describing his hypothesis that job factors had a significant effect on stress. He described the research design, which he had employed in four other companies, that he proposed to employ at Comp Graf. There were no questions during Simon's initial presentation. Following his presentation of the research design (see earlier description), Simon's research assistant described the questionnaire and other measures that would be used to assess job stress and stress outcomes. The questionnaire was distributed to the group. It was the same one used in four previous studies and the research assistant emphasized the extensive work that had gone into developing a reliable and valid instrument. The research assistant further discussed the theoretical and practical rationale for the variables measured by the instrument.

The meeting was then opened for questions and answers. There was a period of uncomfortable silence. Then Long asked Jones to give his views of the study. Jones supported the study on the grounds that, as he said, "We need some help figuring out why we all work so hard and get so little in the way of results. Morale in my organization is really poor." Simon recalls several managers in the room looking at each other and grimacing. Jones then asked several other managers, who appeared to be his subordinates (Simon later found out they were product managers reporting to Jones), to comment on the study. One product manager said that the research results would help if they reduced stress. The other product managers supported this view.

McMulty then asked the other vice presidents what they thought about the research proposal. Several cautiously said that the study might be interesting. Said one, "We will certainly learn something." The vice president of finance asked how much the study would cost and who was to pay for it. Simon, looking at Long, answered that he thought it had been understood from the beginning that if there were to be a study, it would be funded by the company. The vice president of customer service asked Simon about his experience and background. Simon responded by telling him that he had a Ph.D., the kind of research he had been doing in the other companies, some of his findings, and the publications he had to his credit in the field of stress. Others asked some clarifying questions about several items in the questionnaire. In one or two instances they offered some questions to which they thought it would be interesting to have the answer. Simon typically responded to these suggestions by saying that his study depended on standardization in the questionnaire and research design across companies.

It was at this point that Dave Bertram, the manufacturing vice president, asked a pointed question that Simon remembered solicited head nods from the vice presidents of finance and engineering:

> What do you know about our company and its problems? You haven't even been around to talk to us about our business and you are proposing a study that has questionable practical value. You may get a book out of it, but how is it going to solve our backlog problem? Manufacturing and engineering wouldn't have to work those long hours if we had better direction. This study will just add to our workload at a time when we are all pressed.

Simon was surprised by this sudden turn in the meeting and struggled to formulate a response. Just as he was ready to respond, McMulty entered the conversation by saying that the question of direction was an important one but not related to Simon's research program. Simon remembered feeling a sense of relief at the rescue by McMulty. McMulty then went on to say that, "If all of you in the room had a chance to meet with George individually you might see the value of the study to you personally." Looking at Long, he said, "I think Dave (Bertram) is right about George needing to talk to everyone. Why don't you set up a meeting for George with everyone. You are the coordinator for this project." The meeting ended with Long telling everyone that he would call them to set up appointments for Simon.

After the meeting McMulty got Simon and Long aside and reiterated his support for the study. He indicated that he wanted the study because it might help relieve a lot of tension in the company. "Look at me, I'm going to my office now and I'll probably be there until 10 or 11 p.m. I call that work overload, don't you, George?"

MEETINGS WITH KEY PERSONNEL

In the week that followed the meeting, Long and Simon talked on the phone several times. Long related that in talking to several of the people in the meeting he heard a number of concerns. First, the group felt that the questionnaire was far too long and would take too much time away from important work. Second, they had been alienated by the rather academic presentation of research design and questionnaire description. They all agreed that stress was a problem at Comp Graf, but they did not know how the study would help solve the problems at hand. Finally, they seemed to be concerned about what role Simon would play. Would he be a consultant? How would the results be implemented? Would the data be confidential? What form would the feedback take? Long added that he made appointments with about ten key people. He said, "When you talk to them directly, I am sure they will be sold on the research, and you will know a lot more about our problems."

During January, Simon and his research assistant met individually with the people who had been at the meeting. In each meeting they again presented their plan for the study. This time, however, they emphasized that while individual responses were confidential, they planned to aggregate their data, and feed it back to McMulty and his staff so that plans for implementing a stress reduction program could be developed. As he finished on the implementation note, several of the people he talked to volunteered that they knew why there was stress at Comp Graf. Simon did not have to push very hard to get them talking. The following are some of the problems they described.

(1) *Trust was a major concern around Comp Graf.* Nearly all the vice presidents criticized other executives. According to one vice president:

> We've developed strict territories around here, we stay out of each other's departments mostly because we don't trust or approve of what the other guy is doing. I'd like to question someone on their department's activities, but I'd have to let them do it to me. I am not sure I want that.

Apparently, these feelings were particularly true between marketing, engineering and manufacturing. It was not unusual for Jim Ardmore (vice president, engineering) and Dave Bertram (vice president, manufacturing) to blame each other for missed deadlines. As a result, they did not pool information when that was needed to solve problems. No one felt Fred McMulty would listen to these problems. Product managers felt that the lack of trust between functions permeated the whole organization and made it difficult for them to manage their business.

(2) *Lack of planning and confusion was thought to be a problem.* One commonly held feeling was that no one at Comp Graf was skillful enough to plan for the company's future. Each vice president had confidence in the organization's technical competence, but felt that no one was really in touch with the market place and realistic enough to make some good planning decisions for the business. One vice president explained:

> We are all, except Dave Bertram (vice president, manufacturing) relatively new at managing. We are probably experts in our own

area, but because we don't really trust each other, we don't pool information. That kind of coordination isn't the norm around here. Another reason for the confusion is that the company may have outgrown whatever managerial skills and planning skills some of us had.

One major focus of planning criticism was the marketing department.

We haven't figured out what's happening in the market place. Our competitors seem to know. Our sales are dropping and we've been eating away at our backlog. The vice president of marketing had made some real blunders that especially affect engineering and manufacturing. He'd talk to a customer, find out what the customer wanted, and promise a system. That would have been a good move except sometimes the product wasn't designed or produced yet. There are real doubts about marketing's competence.

(3) *Decision making and unmaking was also a complaint that related to the earlier comments.* Apparently no one, particularly Fred McMulty, was willing to take a stand on the long-range issues. But sometimes when Fred McMulty did, it would be quickly reversed. One vice president said:

Sometimes these bimonthly meetings are more confusing than not having them at all. Sometimes we talk for eight hours and leave without a sense of direction. Sometimes we leave with a clear decision, communicate to our subordinates, and then find out later that Fred has changed the policy.

(4) *Shortage of people was a major complaint.* It was not uncommon for people to hold down two and sometimes three jobs, often acting in both supervisory and technical capacities. When we do get new people we have trouble assimilating them. The following comments were typical:

We never have enough people. Everybody works 60 to 80 hours a week. After a while it really gets to you, especially since the pay isn't that great.

I go through a hundred resumes a day. So do other people here, including some line managers. Our whole department is constantly involved in recruiting and hiring. And that's not necessarily good, because we neglect other duties like training and organizational development activities. But even though we are so focused on just recruiting, we still do not bring people in as quickly as many of our line managers want. To get the kind of engineers we need, for example, it usually takes us six months. In the company I worked for 10 years ago, which wasn't growing very fast at all, six months for hiring was fine. Here it's not. Our engineering vice president says the strain we put on his department by hiring so slowly is enormous.

Our new recruits out of college can sometimes get lost in here. We had one last year that nearly cost us a $200,000 order because he was not trained or being supervised closely.

(5) *Problems caused by expanding job demands were cited by several people as causes of stress.* There were comments about shouting matches between various levels regarding questions of delegation and development.

A middle-level manager: The biggest problem we have in this company is top management's unwillingness to delegate more. My boss is still making the same kinds of decisions in the same ways he did five years ago. But the company today is three times as large as it was then. He should be doing other things today and delegating many of those decisions to me.

A top manager: Our biggest problem today is somehow getting middle management to the point where they can handle their ever-increasing responsibilities. I'm still making some decisions that I should not be making. But I have no qualified person beneath me to whom I can delegate those decisions.

A middle-level manager: Top management says that we are not ready to handle more delegation. But how are we ever going to get ready if they don't allow us to make some of those decisions. Sure we would probably make a few errors, but we would learn a lot in the process.

A top manager: We can't afford mistakes around here. We cannot take chances with the record of success we have had here.

There were also comments about the inability of people to grow with jobs and the guilt this problem creates. McMulty said:

> Bob was my fourth employee. I hired him in 1966 to be my first full-time salesman. He worked long hours for us and got two key contracts that saved the company in 1967.
>
> When we hired our seventh salesman, I made Bob sales manager. And in 1971, I made him vice president for sales. Today, in 1980, we have revenues of $100 million on a yearly basis, the marketing department has nearly 100 employees, and Bob is way over his head.
>
> In retrospect, I should never have made him vice president of sales in 1971. But he expected the title change, since I had just made my engineering manager the vice president of engineering. And I didn't want to hurt his feelings or make him think I didn't fully appreciate the loyalty and long hours he had given the company.
>
> Today his inability to manage his department is hurting us severely, but I have delayed moving him for months. I know I have to act soon. But God, it's hard. I really think that as much as I love my wife, throwing her out of the house would not be as emotionally demanding.

(6) *Stress was mentioned by almost everyone as a problem.* One of Comp Graf's engineers took a terminal home so he could work on weekends. The "Comp Graf way of doing things," said one manager, was that people put out 150 percent. "With years and years of experience," he said, "you get to know how to handle pressure." Others saw more difficulties. The vice president of engineering: "We're not the kind of top-down organization where you can pass your problems up the line." One result, as observed by Long, the personnel manager, was extremely high levels of personal stress, job stress, and relocation stress.

Simon emerged from his discussions with executives at Comp Graf with a better knowledge of the individuals and the organizational problems, but unsure about how his research related to the problems. To be sure, Comp Graf would provide an interesting fifth company in his sample since there were clearly many symptoms of stress, and they seemed to relate in part to job factors. But how would the study help in implementing an action program? He remembered feeling overwhelmed. It was already the end of January and he was behind schedule if he was to write up his research in 1981.

CONDUCTING THE RESEARCH

After several discussions with Long and another meeting with McMulty, it was agreed that Simon should proceed with the research. McMulty seemed to be for it. Long felt that the meetings Simon had with key people had gone a long way to establish rapport. Simon felt that his research design would get into some of the issues raised by the people he talked to. Though he discussed what he had heard with Long, he did not discuss his conversations with McMulty. He was concerned that such a discussion would only make the president defensive. Similarly, McMulty did not want another meeting with Simon. McMulty was concerned about time pressures. He reiterated that Long was the coordinator and was to set up the data collection process.

In March 1980, Long and Simon agreed on the following approach given the concerns that had been raised in one-to-one meetings and in the staff meeting.

(1) The questionnaire would be expanded to include some of the issues suggested by the managers as responsible for stress. This lengthened the questionnaire to some 250 items.
(2) A pilot study would be conducted to pretest the questionnaire, check the time that it took to complete it, and so on.
(3) A memo would be written by Long to all 500 salaried and professional people prior to administration of the questionnaire. The memo would explain the rationale of the project, the timing, and commit to feedback to all employees.

(4) The researchers would meet with each functional group in a large meeting to explain the study and develop a sense of ownership for the study.

(5) Feedback would begin within three months and would start at the top.

THE QUESTIONNAIRE

Due to the large number of comments about the ever-changing nature of the business, trust, coordination, and other problems that people felt caused stress, several other scales were added to the questionnaire. In a few instances items were constructed based on the interviews conducted. Arrangements were made to obtain medical data from medical records. This work took two months.

PREPARATION MEETINGS

During the week leading up to the administration of the questionnaire, the researchers visited with each functional work group (from 50 to 150 people) to familiarize them with the research project and to answer any questions. Five points were covered in these sessions.

(1) the purpose of the study—research and implementation;
(2) the kind of questions that would be asked and the confidentiality of the responses;
(3) the researchers' commitment to feedback of results throughout the organization;
(4) the need for people to identify themselves on the questionnaire so that medical data might be obtained to match questionnaire data (it was stressed that this would not be shared with anyone in the company and that individuals who were concerned could talk to the researchers); and
(5) procedural details.

Simon and his research assistant were intentionally vague in their discussion of the questionnaire's contents and about their hypotheses so as not to bias responses. They were also vague about their plans for feedback and implementation because they did not want to raise expectations about possible action even though they hoped for some. According to Simon, "The purpose of the meetings was to increase trust and avoid misconceptions about our intentions." Simon and his associate found that in most meetings people asked few questions. Occasionally, people asked about commitment at the top. Only in the marketing group, where Bob Jones enthusiastically introduced the researchers, were there extensive questions. Most of these centered on how the data would be used.

On the eve of questionnaire administration, a letter signed by McMulty was distributed to all salaried personnel. In it McMulty reiterated his interest in the study, the importance of creating a good work environment, and his commitment to "support the positive use of this information for the benefit of the company and its people." Employees were also informed of the feedback schedule to top management and to each functional group.

QUESTIONNAIRE ADMINISTRATION

On July 1, some 7 months after first proposing the project to management, the questionnaire was administered. It was delivered to contact people in each functional group with instructions for distribution at the end of the working day. Participants were asked to complete the questionnaire at home, away from the distractions of work, and return it in a sealed envelope the following morning. This arrangement had been decided on when several vice presidents objected that asking employees to fill out questionnaires at work would interrupt an already pressured work schedule. Simon had expected the questionnaire to take about an hour and a half to complete and found his predictions accurate with no complaints of it being too time consuming. Within two weeks, 90 percent of the questionnaires were returned. When all questionnaires were in hand, a letter was sent to each participant thanking him for his conscientious involvement, reminding him of the feedback commitment, and reinforcing an earlier point that data interpretation would come largely from the organization itself.

QUESTIONNAIRE ANALYSIS

Data from the questionnaire were analyzed by computer at Simon's university. During this period there was no contact between Simon and executives of Comp Graf except for phone calls with Long. Scale reliabilities, intercorrelations, and regressions against criterion variables were calculated, as were means and frequency distributions for each item and scale. Simon and his associates decided to arrange the data by the percentage of favorable responses on each scale and item. Favorable was interpreted by them as anything that reduced stress or increased harmony. For example, reports of cooperation or normal workload were interpreted as favorable. These data were displayed on transparencies for presentation. Similarly, correlations with criterion variables such as feelings of stress or physiological data were also put on transparencies for presentation. In all there were many transparencies and much data. Because they wanted executives at Comp Graf to interpret their own data and they were not always sure of the meaning of the data themselves, Simon and his associates reported on almost all of the analysis they had performed.

THE DATA FEEDBACK PROCESS

By October 1, three months after administration of the questionnaire and nine months after their meeting with McMulty and his staff, Simon and his associate were ready for feedback to top management. The feedback meeting did not take place until November 3, however, because of difficulties in scheduling. Long reported to Simon that Comp Graf's third quarter was very bad. Backlog was now down to $10 million and cash flow was becoming a real problem. Apparently, there had been several major problems of coordination between marketing, engineering, and manufacturing that resulted in lost orders or orders that were difficult to design and manufacture. As Long said, "The pressure is really on now, and your data about stress should really be relevant."

FEEDBACK TO THE TOP GROUP

On November 3, Simon and his research associate arrived at Comp Graf for the feedback meeting. They had been scheduled to meet with McMulty in the morning to give him an overview of their findings. On a number of job dimensions such as quantitative and qualitative overload as well as some of the other scales they added for Comp Graf, scores were less favorable than in other companies. There was evidence of considerable ambiguity, a scale they had added after their interviews, and they wanted to discuss these findings with McMulty so he would not be surprised. Due to a last-minute customer problem, McMulty was unable to meet with them. The feedback meeting was scheduled from 1 to 5 p.m. in the board room of Comp Graf. Unable to see McMulty, Simon spent the morning with Long, sharing some of his findings. As they talked, the marketing vice president dropped by and became involved in the discussion. He found the role-ambiguity findings very interesting. "I have been telling my colleagues that the marketing role is misunderstood. Now maybe they'll believe me."

When the meeting convened at 1 p.m., Simon found himself at the head of the table. McMulty had been asked to say a few words at the beginning of the meeting, but was called away by a telephone call just before the meeting. McMulty asked Long to start, and Long introduced the feedback process by reminding everyone of how the study got started. He then expressed confidence that the company would benefit from it.

For about an hour Simon went through a series of overhead transparencies that summarized the findings (corporate-wide frequency distributions and means as well as correlations and regressions), being careful not to interpret results or make specific recommendations. Shortly after Simon started, McMulty returned and took a chair near the door. Two vice presidents were called out to the telephone during the presentation. Following the presentation, Simon opened the meeting for discussion. He hoped, he said, that "we can identify some of the key problems causing stress in the organization and develop an action plan for solving them." With that he sat down.

There was silence followed by some questions about the meaning of certain items. A few people complained about the format of the questions and the ambiguity of the feedback scores. "What do these scores mean?" Simon pointed out that Comp Graf was lower on several scales than other companies and that this was at least worthy of noting. The manufacturing vice president dismissed much of the data as either irrelevant or peripheral to the real problem of the company. "I said it before and I'll say it again. What does all this mean to our backlog?" Jones (the marketing vice president) countered that he had talked with Simon earlier and found the role-ambiguity scores interesting. "I think they help explain the problems we in marketing are having." Ardmore (the engineering vice president) countered that "the problem is with your (marketing's) willingness to promise the moon, not ambiguity about your role." Looking to McMulty he said, "We need direction, more structure, and more planning here or we are going to fail." McMulty interrupted to say that he thought tempers were hot because everyone was under pressure and that the research findings were not that controversial. He suggested a coffee break and that the meeting be started again at 3 p.m. Simon agreed that this was a good idea.

During the break McMulty told Simon that he was uncomfortable with the way the meeting was going and that he should have been told in advance about the findings. Before Simon could remind McMulty that a meeting to brief him had been scheduled in the morning, McMulty said, "I hope we can stay with the data and the stress problem after the break."

When the meeting reconvened, tempers had cooled. A number of individuals, however, continued to take issue with the data. Some were skeptical of the value of the feedback data because they disagreed with the way Simon had labeled certain responses —favorable or unfavorable. Said the vice president of finance, "How do we know that role ambiguity is unfavorable? I think it's part of our business. This is only of academic interest." Simon then tried to get the group talking about why people felt their jobs demanded more than they were capable of and what might be done about it. This discussion went on to the rapid rate of growth that was causing rapid promotion. The manager of customer service then said, "Are you suggesting we stop growing at 50 percent a year?" Everyone laughed and looked to McMulty. On several occasions one or another of the vice presidents (except the marketing vice president) suggested that "we already know our problem and don't need a questionnaire to tell us what they are."

The longer the meeting went on, the more the data, the questionnaire, and Simon came under attack. A tendency to argue about variable definition through an item-by-item review of a given dimension developed. Frequently, someone would choose to discount certain data because he felt specific items relating to a variable were either invalid, misinterpreted by employees, or not clear. Simon made every effort to avoid questionnaire dissection in favor of focus and findings but found himself yielding to zealous group members. The more Simon asked the group to talk about underlying problems and actions the more they asked *him* for interpretations.

Time ran out before these difficulties could be resolved. McMulty thanked Simon and suggested that everyone had to think over his report. As the meeting broke up Long reminded everyone around the table that each of their departments had been promised feedback of findings and that he would be scheduling those in November and early December.

Simon was frustrated and upset as he left the meeting. He had provided the data, but the group just did not want to deal with issues. He was apprehensive about the remaining feedback meetings.

FEEDBACK TO THE FUNCTIONAL DEPARTMENTS

Several of the vice presidents resisted strongly Long's efforts to schedule feedback meetings for their groups. Only Jones (marketing vice president) was eager to have one. Only three of the five vice presidents (engineering, marketing, and finance) could find the time to schedule a feedback meeting in November or December.

Each feedback meeting was attended by the salaried people who had participated in the study. This meant the groups ranged in size from 25 in finance to over 100 in engineering. Simon and his associate used the same statistical breakdowns and overheads (corporate means, distributions, correlations and regressions) they had used in the presentation to McMulty and his staff. Each feedback meeting was scheduled for two hours.

The meeting typically started with an introduction by the vice president in charge, a brief update of the origin of the study by Long, and the presentation by Simon. However, only the marketing vice president introduced Simon with any degree of enthusiasm.

Simon began each presentation by saying that his research at Comp Graf had uncovered some interesting findings about the level of stress in the company compared to others he had studied, and that job factors, his main focus of interest, definitely seemed to be related to this stress. He said he was hopeful that a program could be implemented to modify the job factors that had been causing stress, and that perhaps a personal stress management program might also be the answer. "I hope," he said, "that these meetings will stimulate you to do what you can in your own areas." During feedback in the engineering department (the first presentation) someone spoke out and asked, "What did people at the top say when you fed back this data to them? Are they going to do something about it? They are the ones who are causing all the stress around here." Except for head nods from several others who seemed to agree, there was silence in the room. Simon then said that he was not sure what the outcome would be but that the top group was thinking about the data and he was reasonably sure that they would try to take some action. "Fred McMulty is very concerned about stress in the company," said Simon.

The remainder of the meeting in engineering was like the other two meetings. On several occasions, disagreements surfaced in the audience about the interpretation of an item. It became clear that people had somewhat different views of what they were responding to. This then led to some questioning about the validity of the items. But the question about what action top management would take was a recurring theme. Others wanted to know if there were separate breakdowns for engineering, marketing, and other departments. A few supervisors wondered whether they might be able to get data breakdowns for their particular groups. Simon promised to provide these to a half dozen or so supervisors who asked for this breakdown. At least this was encouraging, he thought. Someone is interested.

JANUARY 1, 1981: REFLECTIONS

It was the experience of the previous year with research at Comp Graf that prevented Simon from enjoying the holiday season. Why had research on stress in an organization that obviously had a lot of it fail to stimulate an action program? What, if anything, should be done now? What should he do about the half dozen or so supervisors that wanted data on their groups? Jones in marketing was interested in doing something about stress and was looking to Simon for recommendations about how the research might be utilized in his department. Should he follow up, and if he did, what impact would that have on his relationship with the other departments at Comp Graf? He was particularly concerned about the call from McMulty. Should he call to follow up or should he wait for McMulty's call? He knew that Long would be calling him. What should he say to him?

These and many other questions, to which he did not have answers, bothered Simon. But one problem bothered him more than any other. He knew that the promise of using the data to improve the atmosphere at Comp Graf and decrease employee stress had been one of the main reasons that McMulty, Long, and Jones had supported the project to begin with. Now, however, although he had data for his writing projects, Simon knew that his heart was no longer in that commitment to help Comp Graf implement change.

5

Turning Knowledge into Application

Gaining Resources for Research and Implementation

ORGANIZATIONAL ENVIRONMENTS AND KEY ISSUES

Research for implementation is far more likely to be successful if it accounts for or if it anticipates the environment, including environmental factors external to or beyond the control of either the researcher or the organization. It is often useful to design research in some kind of contemporary frame—to introduce a notion of urgency or importance—otherwise there is little incentive for others to contribute to or support this research.

Every organizational environment includes a set of issues that must be addressed. While these issues may vary among businesses, among industries, among companies, and across years or decades, the researcher will find it advantageous to identify the issues relevant to the environment in which research is planned. For example, key issues for a businss might include: inflation, productivity, innovation, an aging work force, people to be managed, and corporate image. These are not the only key issues. This list is simply illustrative and researchers should be encouraged to develop or identify the key issues that are appropriate for their projects.

There are some consequences and implications of inadequate attention to key issues. For example, if inflation is ignored by a company, the probable results will include: salary compression and the subsequent loss of the incentive value of money; the motivation to excel will be dampened, and the company's ability to attract or compete for outstanding people is thus reduced.

If productivity and innovation are ignored as issues, the following results are likely: creativity will not sustain itself because it requires direction and management; productivity will not be sustained without new ideas; growth will not be possible because innovation is absent; and without a climate for innovation, outstanding people will leave, mediocre ones will remain, and another motivational incentive will be lost.

Ignoring an aging workforce has other implications. These include a workforce characterized by longer individual assignments, the frustrations of severe salary compression, motivational problems, job terminations, and deadend careers. A company's ability to deal with these problems is often limited because of the current climate for and laws of "entitlement," e.g., people feel "entitled" to a job, "entitled" to good pay, "entitled" to promotion. Ignoring some of the issues or problems involved with an aging workforce will often result in the departure of career-blocked people and lawsuits based on age discrimination.

Further, the issue of corporate image is important. If ignored, a company will have difficulty attracting employees as well as the investment community. A company's image on campus, with the investment community, and with its employees must be developed, enhanced, and sustained. Unless image is developed and maintained, an organization will suffer severe consequences.

Researchers who show an awareness of such environmental issues and their implications are more likely to be working within the reality system of a client organization. Importantly, recognition of these issues will enhance the researcher's credibility and his or her ability to obtain more organization interest in prospective research. A researcher must be able to show a relationship between relevant issues and proposed research objectives.

MANAGEMENT SPONSORSHIP OF RESEARCH

Researchers have more than one kind of audience or sponsor for research findings. Generally, innovative researchers have something in common. They usually start with a problem and have something of a vision or "mind picture" of what might solve the problem. They see the whole thing at once. Naturally, not all the details are worked out and that requires subsequent work, but the solution is often there from the beginning. These researchers often go from problem to solution without going through all the logical-deductive thinking normally associated with the scientific method. In fact, they usually do not follow the scientific method initially. Scientific method is followed only to test their assumptions and to put some meat on the bones of their original idea. What those researchers tend *not* to do is to follow the scientific method and do theory testing in hopes of coming up with a solution to a problem bit by bit and piece by piece.

After their initial hunch, the next most common characteristic of these researchers is their persistence. Persistence requires convincing others of their idea to solicit help, funding, and suggestions. Basically, they look for reinforcement. Another way to look at it is that successful innovators create self-fulfilling prophecies. The reality is, however, that prophecies do not fulfill themselves—they require a good deal of persuading and selling. This latter point is often viewed by scientists as "unworthy"of their effort. In no way, however, do "innovative" researchers reject the use of traditional scientific methodology—they just do not often use it to conceive or promote an idea.

Since innovation is usually followed closely by resistance to change, the notion of being above the need to "sell" an idea, or that selling is somehow morally wrong, is probably inappropriate for an applied scientist. Persuading, it seems, is generally considered appropriate for a parent, teacher, friend, spouse, manager, politician, or business executive. In reality, it is also appropriate and necessary for applied behavioral scientists.

One alternative to applied research is the systematic accumulation of information, bit by bit, in laboratory situations. Advocates of this approach admit that this might only add up to the equivalent of "an inch" in a lifetime but at least it would provide reliable information. An inch in a lifetime amounts to perhaps a foot in a number of generations. We need to move faster than that on some problems, or the only people who will exchange this information will be the scientists themselves, with a miniscule impact. While the scientific method is, of course, absolutely vital and even more important than a "leap-frogging" process of development, there is still a need for leap-frogging. Leap-frogging must also be followed by classical methodology as a means of confirming and / or qualifying an unusual observation or conclusion—otherwise it would be too easy to leap-frog off a cliff.

Is there a need, therefore, for "tactical communications"? Is "selling" wrong? Can research with implementation in mind properly account for leap-frogging? Conducting research with implementation in mind cannot proceed in a vacuum; it must account for both insight and relevant aspects of the organization's environment.

GAINING SKILL IN COMMUNICATING WITH MANAGERS

The materials in this chapter are best used in a workshop in which you can play roles as researcher and manager. The materials have two purposes:

(1) *To create an awareness of the questions that the researcher should ask of managers and should expect from managers.* For

example, the researcher should focus questions on the client's operational objectives, identification of initial source of interest or encouragement, who can be counted on for help, probable obstacles, prior attempts, what is "in it" for management if the project is successful, and the consequences if it is unsuccessful. The researcher must also learn to respond to challenges from managers as well as to requests for premature answers or expedient solutions.

(2) *To broaden the competency repertoire of the researcher.* This can be illustrated or accomplished by demonstrating the types of skills necessary to (a) gain management confidence, (b) determine the actual incentives for strong managerial support as well as possible obstacles to support, and (c) show how to involve people in situations to get early tangible results which will permit larger involvement.

Researchers need to be able to converse as fluently with managers as they do among themselves. Managers' language and concerns are different from researchers', and thus researchers need to be "bilingual."

LEVEL OF SUPPORT AND RESEARCHER CREDIBILITY

Top-level management support is not always necessary. A researcher can start with a level of management that controls the area in which research is planned. The only stipulation is that members of management in that area actually see it in their own self-interest to get information that the study can provide.

Some organizations will participate in research if it is seen as an interesting and possible solution to a problem. Other organizations want something more tangible. In any case, an organization will look for relevance between a potential research outcome and its operating problems. The closer the relationship between research and actual operating problems, the more likely it is that a project will get good support.

When picking a research project for implementation, it should have (a) a good theoretical rationale, (b) previous or related research information that makes the implementation a logical next step, (c) visible and probable short-range potential benefit (one to three years) to the organization.

Researchers should remember that the conduct and outcome of research will impact on their credibility; i.e., a researcher may want to come back to an organization and will be judged not on knowledge of the literature or experimental design, but on (1) communications skills and (2) the actual benefit to an organization. Organizations will take risks, but they should be made aware by the researcher when there are low odds of success. The cost of research should always be balanced against the potential for benefit. Most organizations want a researcher to contribute to the solution of a problem, not to create a greater one.

Researchers should not conduct mundane research just for the sake of getting positive results. This will not impress anyone in management and it will probably not do much for the credibility of the researcher. Instead, the applied researcher should find a way to tie an organization's problem to research interest.

MEASURES

Measures are important. Managers should be asked to identify pre and post measures that would be most convincing to them. Prior to embarking on a study, a researcher should ask managers "what if" questions to understand better how they might react to various pre and post changes in experimental variables, e.g., "What if there is a 5 percent increase/25 percent increase?"; "How much of the increase can be attributed to things other than the experimental manipulation?" Researchers should remember that the cost of getting an improvement may not be an acceptable cost. For example, a researcher might be able to bring about a 28 percent improvement in an important variable while the cost of doing it might be inordinately (unacceptably) high. Managers should be questioned for their opinions on cost/benefit comparisons for proposed research.

When talking with managers, there is a skill in analyzing a situation to determine where interests and obstacles exist. Communicating objectives and encouraging participation is another skill. An applied researcher must be optimistic about outcomes without promising results or overstating the likelihood or benefits of successful research.

SKILLS IN TWO CONTEXTS

There are two major contexts for enacting communications and tactical skills: (1) when *being asked by managers* for problem-solving assistance and (2) when *approaching managers* for the purpose of persuading them to give a green light to a research project. Moreover, these discussions will be conducted with two levels of management: high-level management (policymaking) and/or operating-level management. Both levels have different interests and needs, sometimes requiring skills to be enacted differently. This will be evident during the role playing, as described below. "Learning points" are provided for each listed skill to guide you in the execution of that skill. Each point must be carefully followed or the interaction is not likely to be successful.

FORMAT FOR INSTRUCTION

The communications skills of an applied researcher can be improved with practice. Quality of practice will depend upon the range of issues and obstacles introduced. It is prudent to develop these skills prior to attempting research in an actual organizational environment. Perhaps the best format to develop communication skills is by using behavior modeling, i.e., role play (skill practice) structured about behaviorally specific "learning points."

Researchers should exchange roles during skill practice since learning will take place from both sides. Individuals taking the roles of managers should ask questions that range from cynicism and disinterest through defensiveness to genuine interest. Individuals in the managerial role should also include questions to see if the researcher "oversells" research potential, thereby sacrificing long-term relationships for short-term research outcome.

The two situational contexts identified previously should be the starting points, i.e., (1) situations in which the psychologist is asked by management for help on a problem and (2) situations in which the psychologist approaches management with a proposal. Each role play should be limited to 10 to 15 minutes.

Skills to be improved or learned are listed below. Each skill has a set of "learning points" associated with it. At various times during the role plays, the researcher will have opportunities to listen and react, explain the rationale for a project, defend an idea, redirect management's expressed interest or objectives, identify one's own research competence, get agreement and commitment, explain research methodology, express an opinion, question existing practices, and, of course, introduce a new idea. Researchers will learn that as many as possible of these skills should be implemented in a discussion with management.

Taking about 5 or 10 minutes to prepare for a role play is probably useful. Role plays should be critiqued by the individuals in both roles (researcher and manager) as well as by others who are observing. Critiques should be based only on how well the learning points were enacted. The learning points must be the primary criterion against which skills are observed and evaluated. The evaluation should take place after each role play in the form of oral comment by observers and participants.

The situations enacted in each role play are designed to provide illustrations of certain situations and to enable experience with some of the "learning points." As an outcome of the role plays, researchers will learn the tactical importance of using learning points systematically and appropriately.

 Prior to each role play, participants should pay particular attention to the context in which an interaction takes place, e.g., hostile or benign, large versus small, when requested to do research versus requesting to do it.

Following the learning points is crucial. This is not an attempt to program a researcher; instead, following these learning points should result in broader competence and more flexibility on the researcher's part.

LEARNING POINTS

(A) *Explaining the Rationale for a Project* (to show "what's in it" for management)
  (1) Concisely describe in nontechnical terms the primary and secondary objectives of the project and the advantages of conducting it with the methodology you suggest.
  (2) Ask for and listen to management's reaction.
  (3) Explain how project findings will benefit the sponsoring managers and their organization—and contrast these benefits with the consequences or implications of not completing the project.
  (4) Ask for and respond to questions by restating points 1 and 3 (if appropriate) and express your appreciation for their support.

(B) *Listening and Reacting* (to show understanding and to generate confidence in the researcher)
  (1) Tell the manager that you are especially interested in learning his or her personal opinion about the project/problem.
  (2) Ask the manager to describe how his or her personal or organization effectiveness might be influenced by the project and/or problem; listen openly.
  (3) Do not respond to the manager's comments with objections; instead, ask the manager to elaborate on those points where you may disagree and discuss your own views.

.

    (4) When you terminate a conversation, thank the manager for his or her views and tell him or her that you will consider them before proceeding with the project.

    (5) If appropriate, set a specific follow-up date to redefine the project or get agreement.

(C) *Defending or Presenting an Idea, Opinion, or Project* (to show professional competence and ability to contribute to management objectives)

    (1) Express your opinion and explain why you hold it versus other alternatives

    (2) In tangible terms, describe the relationship between your idea/project/proposal and management objectives as you understand them.

    (3) Ask for and listen to management's reaction.

    (4) Do not indicate objection to points with which you disagree, but ask managers to explain their reasons.

    (5) Discuss and compare your opinion and management's in reference to the best criteria you can identify for measuring management's objectives.

(D) *Redirecting or Redefining Management's Expressed Interest or Objectives* (to ensure that research results will be useful and to make sure that the research answers the questions that management should be raising)

    (1) Express your understanding of management's interests and objectives and suggest a more fundamental perspective together with your reasons for offering it.

    (2) In tangible terms, explain the relationship between your more fundamental perspective and management's need.

    (3) Ask for and discuss management's reaction to your recommendation.

    (4) If necessary, briefly outline how management's interest or objectives will be met by following a more fundamental recommendation.

(E) *Identifying One's Own Research Competence and Ability to Get Results* (because not all researchers are equally well suited in all areas)

(1) Consider the independent and dependent variables involved and compare your knowledge of these variables and experience with manipulating or measuring them.

(2) Is this research area intrinsically interesting to you—or is it likely to be boring if you seek replication?

(3) List the names of several other researchers you know who are probably better qualified to study the problem—decide whether to suggest another resarcher for the project.

(4) If the research is unsuccessful, would you find ways to explore these variables?

(F) *Getting Agreement and Commitment* (to make sure that management understands what it must do to provide support and follow-up)

(1) Review with management the rationale of the project.

(2) Indicate and discuss specific responsibilities, tasks, milestones, and deadlines for management.

(3) Ask for and discuss their reactions.

(4) Tell the managers you will summarize the schedule and actions in writing and submit these to them for their record.

(5) Set specific follow-up dates with management to review progress at each milestone.

(G) *How to Question an Existing Practice*

(1) Briefly explain your concern.

(2) Ask why an alternative practice (stated or unstated) is not being considered.

(3) Respond with your reasons for questioning the existing practice.

(4) Give your suggestion for an alternative practice and why you think it more effectively meets management needs (if your sugestion is not thoroughly worked out, present it in outline with a request for time and suggestions to develop it further).

(H) *How to Introduce a New Idea*

(1) Identify the individuals who are most likely to resist your idea.

(2) In a nonthreatening way, describe your idea and say that you would appreciate their reaction to it. Listen openly.

(3) If necessary, restate why you think your idea is a good one and how management would benefit from its adoption.

(4) Tell management that you would welcome help in developing and testing the idea.

INTRODUCTION TO ROLE PLAY EXERCISES

It is often useful for someone knowledgeable about the details of managment "problems" to assume the role of management in these exercises. If workshops are conducted, a workshop staff member will play the role of manager in the first role play (the motivation problem) to illustrate how this should be done. In the remaining role plays, participants should be asked to play both roles (i.e., researcher and manager) because they will learn something about both sides of the interaction. The workshop staff should guide and critique the role plays.

SITUATION 1: A MOTIVATION PROBLEM (REQUEST FROM MANAGEMENT)

Productivity is low, and the manager wants more dedication from employees and wants to know how they can be motivated to do more. *Middle management* feels that some in-house research or even available knowledge might identify things to do and/or areas to probe to bring about this result, i.e., more dedication and more motivation with a resultant impact on productivity. During the role play, the researcher should be prepared to discuss measures, past research, new research design, myths, and target groups. This, of course, should not preclude other things that should be discussed, e.g., top management support or union relations.

Here is an example of role play detail to structure the exercise: An electronics manufacturer, a division of a major company, employs day-rate labor in a union shop. The tasks are not belt-paced but are an electronics parts-assembly job centered around individual work stations. Productivity is 15 percent below time standards. Quality (rejects) should be .05 percent but runs about 3 percent. These figures have represented a decline in plant performance for the past three months. Previously performance had been at levels indicated by time standards but have eroded to their present level and there is concern that they will continue to erode.

The manager of manufacturing, reporting to the plant manager, has been getting a lot of pressure to improve productivity. His personnel manager has urged him to look for some consulting help. Therefore, he has asked the psychologist to tell him how to improve productivity. In fact, he will be grateful if he can learn anything that will be useful to him.

SITUATION 2: SELECTION/MANAGEMENT SUCCESSION (REQUEST FROM MANAGEMENT)

In this situation, *top management* is not happy with the quality of managers being hired from outside. Too many of them are not effective nor is management happy with the relatively few good people inside the company who are available for promotion. Top management has no confidence in the flow of people internally. Management wants a program to do a better job of selecting new managers and identifying "high potential" people earlier. Top management wants something done to get people ready for responsibility faster. Management is asking the psychologist/researcher to recommend a program to improve the quality of people selected for management positions, either from the outside or within. The psychologist/researcher is asked to have a set of recommendations in two months and a program in place in eight months.

Here is detail that can be used for this role play: The president of a medium-sized company, who has grown up through the ranks of the company and knows most of the executives, has become very impatient recently. He feels that too many people are being hired from the outside to fill key positions, i.e., individuals reporting directly to the general managers of each of his five divisions. The president claims that these individuals hired from the outside are not, in his opinion, performing at adequate levels based on their performance appraisals and the performance of those divisions. Further, when the president looks at who is available for promotion from inside the company, he observes that there are inadequate numbers of competent people coming along. The development of people is apparently not good, he has concluded. He insists on more accurate early identification of good people and a better way to prepare them for handling more responsibility effectively. Therefore, he wants the psychologist to tell him how to improve the quality of people selected from outside or inside his company. He wants a set of recommendations in two months and a program that can be implemented in eight months. The president insists on a program that works, without concern for the feelings of other executives in the company because they have failed to develop a good management succession process on their own. He wants the psychologist to recommend a program and to assume responsibility for implementing it.

SITUATION 3: DIAGNOSTIC ASSESSMENT AND FOLLOW-UP (APPROACHING MANAGEMENT FOR COOPERATION)

In this situation, the psychologist/researcher wants to introduce a program that will enable prospective managers to be more effective at their tasks. The psychologist is thinking about an assessment center to provide diagnostic information about managerial skills (actual as well as potential) and then following up the assessment with training to address the weaknesses identified by the assessment program. The psychologist feels that a needs analysis probably should be done as a basis for the assessment center as well as for subsequent training for managerial skills. In this situation, *middle management* must be persuaded. The researcher should discuss issues such as validity, predictability, and specific training programs.

For role play detail, the following is suggested: In this situation, the psychologist/researcher wants to introduce a program that will enable prospective managers to be more effective. The psychologist has worked with the staff of this organization for two years and has heard many complaints about the quality of first-level supervision. There are four levels of management in this organization.

The psychologist will recommend an assessment center to provide diagnostic information about managerial skills (actual as well as potential) to assist with the selection of new managers. The psychologist also plans to recommend following assessment with training to address the weaknesses identified by the assessment program. The psychologist feels that this process of assessing managerial competence should focus on problem analysis skills and motivation. However, he or she feels that a "needs analysis" probably should be done prior to designing the assessment center.

Middle management must be persuaded to provide planning funds for preparing a specific project plan.

SITUATION 4: GAINING COOPERATION FOR YOUR PROJECT (APPROACHING MANAGEMENT)

For the Situation 4 role play, attention will be focused on problems selected by participants. Participants will be arranged into groups of three, and each person will rotate through the roles of researcher, manager, and observer.

As the researcher, you will want to introduce a new program or project to the manager, or to resolve a problem in an ongoing project.

Pick a topic that is of personal and professional interest from an area in which you now work or intend to be working in the next year or two. Write out a one- or two-paragraph briefing sheet and bring it to the workshop. The briefing sheet should describe (1) the program, project, or problem, (2) the key manager to whom the presentation will be made, and (3) pertinent background information about the issues relevant to the manager's decision about your project.

Participants should have cleared each problem with the workshop staff prior to this session.

During each role play, researchers should select and use the learning points and other information previously reviewed with their "management." After each role play, the observer will make his or her comments and elicit comments from the "management" as well as from the researcher.

ADDITIONAL ROLE PLAY SITUATIONS

Researchers should construct their own situations, based on their experience, and should practice their skills in these situations. Asking acquaintances in management positions for their ideas about problems to practice is also useful.

CONCLUSION

Role playing is an extremely useful technique for rehearsing for the critical interpersonal encounters that take place in starting and conducting a research project. Despite the power of role playing, most people prefer to perform extemporaneously rather than to rehearse. Perhaps this is so because role playing so easily reveals discrepancies between intended and actual outcomes. Knowing a principle and effectively enacting a sequence of behaviors based on it can be quite different things.

Many principles of effective research and implementation design can be inferred from the first four chapters. This chapter presented some additional principles, in the form of Learning Points. Integrating these diverse principles into effective behavioral sequences for persuading managers requires continuing practice. Unused skills deteriorate, but rehearsal via role playing can minimize the difference between intention and outcome.

6

Making It Happen
Research and Implementation

MANAGEMENT AS A CONTACT SPORT

Almost 100 years ago, Fayol stressed the notion that managers, as administrators, spend considerable time organizing, planning, administering, and controlling the work of others. While probably descriptive of the manager's job at the turn of the century, it is not an accurate portrayal of behaviors in today's executive suite.

A number of recent analyses of managerial behavior show some startling changes. Beginning with the seminal work of Mintzberg (1973), a number of studies (McCall, 1978; Kotter, 1982) have shown that the modern manager's world is characterized by a fragmented workday, with little time for thinking and planning. Action oriented, the modern manager relies on personal networks and contacts for much of the information he or she deals with. Sayles (1980, p. 25) describes this in this manner:

> The managerial workday consists of a never-ending series of contacts with people—talking, listening, telephoning, arguing, and negotiating. A first line supervisor may have hundreds of contacts in a day, many lasting less than a minute; while a slower-paced chief executive may have twenty or thirty. Even at that imposing level, most managerial activities last less than ten minutes. Two European studies found that it was unusual for even chief executives to work on any one thing for as long as a half hour.

Managerial work is hectic and fragmented, requiring the ability to shift continually from person to person and from one problem to the next. It is almost the opposite of the studied, analytical, persisting work pattern of the professional, who expects and demands closure and the time to do a careful and complete job that will provide pride of authorship. While the professional moves logically and sequentially through a work plan, the executive responds to one unanticipated event after another, and even at high levels, is at the mercy of the situation.

Several important features of managerial work need to be understood by the researcher. First, most executives do not have enough time. Action oriented for the most part, their emphasis often is on doing rather than on reflecting. Researchers should be aware of, and prepared for, just a few minutes of interrupted time. Executive summaries highlighting what needs to be done will be more appreciated and will have more impact than a lengthy research proposal.

The initial meeting with a key executive can shape the entire outcome of a project. Careful planning is required. Expect to be interrupted. While you may feel this is rude, it simply reflects the time demands associated with the executive suite.

Since you probably will have only a half hour of interrupted time, visual aids can be very helpful. Generally, only one or two are required. These visual aids should be large enough to be read by several managers at once. Visual aids can structure the presentation if interrupted. Most senior managers respond best to verbal stimuli. If reinforced with a visual aid, the presentation tends to have a greater impact. You are competing with many others for this precious time. You should think of ways to market your ideas and to address the needs of the audience.

It is also very important to use this meeting to obtain whatever resources are needed. Be prepared to make specific requests, e. g., a meeting with other managers to begin implementation of research activities, staff resources, specific next steps, and so on. Successful research implementers respond to the action orientation of managers. Be prepared to answer the question, "What will this do for us?"

There are many other aspects of the managerial role that are important. A good overview of the typical roles associated with many management functions is provided by Mintzberg (1973). One aspect worth singling out, often because it is overlooked, is the extent to which managers rely on and use personal networks. Kotter (1982) points out that senior managers spend the vast majority of their careers in one industry. This tends to create a web of relationships—a network used for information acquisition and dissemination. Senior managers have very effective networks. Managerial work often gets done by verbal exchange, personal contact, and a series of interdependent bargains. The effective researcher should be prepared for this.

Successful implementers should be able to become part of this network. Assume that, if you have something interesting to say, it will be repeated to others. Think how this executive will describe your meeting to others. Try to prepare him or her for this, by summarizing the discussion or by having the executive review what was discussed. Be concrete, but remember the basic rule of effective implementers: Do not promise anything unless you can deliver.

One final perspective is provided by the decor of the office itself. Often a manager's office gives useful clues to the thinking of its inhabitant. McCaskey (1979) has prepared a helpful article describing the hidden messages managers send. Being able to "read" these messages can be a useful guide that too often is overlooked.

ORGANIZATIONAL PRACTICES:
READY, AIM, FIRE OR READY, FIRE, AIM?

Most organizations have ways of doing things that characterize their climates. Obviously, the more a researcher knows about an organization, the easier it will be to translate concepts, terms, and problems from a professional language to the language of the manager.

A number of excellent general professional sources exist. Mintzberg (1981) presents a useful model that describes organizational settings. He points out that many problems in organizational design stem from the assumption that organizations are all alike. He provided a useful model showing how five basic units can be configured differently and its effects on organizational behavior. Levinson's (1972) text on organizational diagnosis describes a number of information-gathering techniques, and Beer's (1981) recent book provides perspective on many contemporary management practices. There are many contributing factors to an organization's climate. Its size, age, history, stage in its life cycle, competition, and markets all help to shape how an organization works.

While there probably are as many differences among organizations as there are differences among people, some organizations work better. Several years ago, McKinsey and Company studied the management practices in 37 different companies that tend to get cited in the popular business literature as examples of well-run organizations (Peters, 1980). Two different criteria were used to identify organizations that were well run. The first criterion was sustained financial performance over an extended period of time —usually a decade or more, focusing on profitability (all were private-sector organizations) and return on equity. The second criterion was based on the organization's reputation as innovative as viewed by peers, competitors, and industry experts. Admittedly, this was not a "scientific" study. Yet, several practices exist which, if adapted by the researcher, could potentially enhance implementation efforts.

Often, these practices are dissimilar to behaviors used by researchers, and the quote taken from Sayles (1980) is worth re-reading here. The most successful managers and successful organizations are action oriented. Their key instructions are pointed, such as "do it, fix it, try it." Successful organizations avoid analyzing products to death, avoid complicated methods to develop new ideas, and approach new ideas by attempting to get some data, rather than waiting for a complete experiment. Generally, ideas are tested quickly—those that work are pushed, those that do not are discarded. At the extreme, these behaviors can be described as "Ready, Fire, Aim," yet the researcher should be prepared to cope with an environment that expects, and demands, results in a very short time frame.

Peters also notes a number of behaviors that, while not used by all the successful organizations studied, appear often enough to warrant mentioning—particularly, as an aid to the researcher in providing information that can be acceptable to a host organization. Significantly, these often can be diametrically opposed to behaviors that lead to successful research not being done with a goal of implementation.

For example, a number of highly successful companies force their managers to write brief, straightforward business memos. One company goes as far as to insist on a one-page memo as its norm. Ideas presented in this format have to be readable with little jargon present. The implication to the researcher/implementer should be obvious.

Many companies use task forces to solve problems. These task forces may be staffed by people who can be "spared," or by people who cannot. Generally, problem-solving (rather than problem-finding) task forces use line managers who cannot be spared. This results in two specific outcomes—problems are task centered and meetings are brief. Again, an implicit message is there for the researcher/implementer.

WHAT THIS ALL BOILS DOWN TO

We all carry stereotypes with us. Managers are no different and their stereotype of the behavioral scientist may or may not be reinforced by what you do. You can maximize your likelihood of success by doing your homework. This means learning as much about the host organization as you can, prior to soliciting its help. Successful managers are good fact finders. They expect to have (and usually get) direct responses to their questions. This often requires the ability to get at the heart of an issue. To the extent that you are able to do efficient (translate that as quick) fact finding, your likelihood for success increases. Getting research implemented requires many skills. It also requires a good understanding of the host organization. It requires good timing, and at times, depends upon luck as well.

There is a variety of "gallows" humor, grim and cynical in its undertones, that is found in many places in which researchers and managers collaborate on projects. A product of such a circumstance is the following stage theory of projects:

The Six Project Stages
(1) Wild Enthusiasm
(2) Disillusionment
(3) Total Confusion
(4) The Search for the Guilty
(5) The Punishment of the Innocent
(6) The Promotion of the Nonparticipants

Successful research *and* implementation seems to be a comparative rarity, regardless of timing and luck. It should be more frequent, and to that end we offer our summary of critical factors.

CRITICAL FACTORS RELATED TO UNSUCCESSFUL IMPLEMENTATION EFFORTS

(1) The researcher was not prepared. He or she did not do his or her homework, did not understand the fundamental research issues, did not anticipate experimental design conditions, did not prepare an adequate presentation, or did not anticipate resistance.
(2) The researcher is unable to give acceptable reasoning for specific

findings, problems related to subjects, methods, and the like.

(3) The management of the organization is too polite and is not really committed to the research issues presented.

(4) Research fails because management inherently is "too ignorant" to understand the dynamics or causes of the problem.

(5) Research fails because management is "_____" (bad, inept, selfish, evil).

(6) Research fails because management only gives lip service to the notion of conducting research but fundamentally has its own ideas for action plans that are totally unrelated to any issues raised by the researcher.

(7) Along with this, management has other priorities that the researcher never addressed.

(8) A key factor may be that time has passed since the development of the original research ideas, and because of this, the actors have changed. The actors here can be key management representatives, subjects, or one's own research staff, i.e., a very talented research assistant leaving midstream in project.

(9) Research fails because the researcher has not done an adequate job of fact finding and consequently has designed a program addressing the wrong needs.

(10) Research fails because management had faulty assumptions and expected miracles to occur when the researcher should have highlighted what he or she was able to deliver.

(11) Research fails because management was too impatient, too insistent, and wanted to implement changes before understanding the causes behind the problem, and so on.

(12) Research fails because managers want instant answers to questions that are not researchable.

(13) Research fails because managers expect researchers to make policy—an area the researcher may be unprepared for or not capable of handling.

(14) Research fails because the problem has changed in the time since research was initiated.

(15) Research fails because the individual studying the problem has not been given all the facts or has not been able to ascertain the relevant facts.

(16) Research fails because the individual is not given enough support.

(17) Research fails because the subjects will not respond; i.e., they are uncooperative, they will not fill out the questionnaires or respond to data collection efforts wholeheartedly.

(18) Research fails because the researcher picked the wrong sponsor.

SUMMARY

Failure is likely to occur when:

- problem identification is incorrect;
- sponsor power is lacking;
- there are changes in needs and/or key personnel;
- the impetus for the project is not clearly specified or it changes;
- there are unrealistic expectations for results or delivery schedules; and/or
- the researcher is insensitive to the social and political dynamics of the organization.

CRITICAL FACTORS RELATED TO SUCCESSFUL IMPLEMENTATION EFFORTS

(1) The ability of the researcher to identify what is in it for whom.

(2) The ability of the researcher to negotiate resources, schedules, and the purposes of the research. This includes discussions of why the research is being done, who sees the results, what implications and interventions may result from research, and so forth.

(3) The ability of the researcher to communicate tangibly with all of the appropriate populations he or she might be dealing with, including policymakers, management supporters, supervisors of subjects, subjects, and so on.

(4) The existence of a letter of agreement or contract that clearly specifies the mutual expectations and obligations of both parties —researcher and client organization. Such a document can be referred to later when (as often happens, particularly when the findings are in and feedback is about to be given) recollections about what was agreed to are found to be discrepant.

(5) The presence of a "liaison group" or "advisory panel," a micro-cosm of the part of the organization in which the study is being done, to monitor how the research is progressing. Such a group can be useful for the researcher in getting questions answered, checking the acceptability of changes that may need to be made in the research plan, pretesting the feedback and designing its format, and so on. It can also be a useful device in bringing unin-tended consequences of the research to the researcher's attention.

(6) The capability to deliver results and project information in a timely and appropriate fashion.

(7) The ability of the researcher to approach various constituencies in a nonpretentious manner, maintaining or enhancing their self-esteem.

(8) The ability of the researcher to admit that he or she may not have all the answers or admit that he or she is wrong when appropriate.

(9) Personal integrity—this implies taking bold, innovative, and somewhat aggressive stances when appropriate.

(10) Technical and professional competence in both understanding the domain of the problem as well as in responding appropriately to professional issues related to ethics, feedback, and so forth.

(11) The ability to respond to issues in a timely fashion.

(12) The ability to anticipate problems as they emerge, and flexibility in dealing with those issues.

(13) Openness to ideas of constituent groups and ability to incorpor-ate them in the research design and implementation plans.

(14) A lack of defensiveness in dealing with problems.

SUMMARY

Successful implementation most often occurs when one is able to:

- identify interests of key persons and constituencies;
- define and negotiate the purposes of the project;
- identify and resolve policy issues up front;
- negotiate adequate resources and schedules;

- make contingency plans;
- model success behaviors; and
- deliver results.

Appendix A

Conducting a Workshop on Research and Implementation

The materials in this monograph were originally prepared as an eight-hour workshop, an ideal medium for their presentation because of the dynamic interchange among participants.

Eight hours is the minimum amount of time to devote to research and implementation issues, but a satisfactory result can be achieved if enough preparation is done in advance. In particular, this means that participants will need to read the entire monograph prior to the session (if two sessions are scheduled a day or more apart, participants should read Chapters 1-4 for the first session and Chapters 5 and 6 for the second).

A nominal timeline for a workshop is given below.

Workshop Schedule

Activity	Minimum Time Needed
Introduction, Overview, and Objectives	30 minutes
Discussion of the Comp Graf Case Study	2-1/2 hours
Demonstration of Implementation Skills in Role Plays	3 hours
Discussion of Issues in Conducting Research and Implementation	2 hours

The time allocated to each of these activities can be greatly increased. For example, if you wish to discuss the items in the Research Style Inventory or the discussion questions that follow the Scoring and Interpretation Guide, the 30 minutes allocated for the Introduction, Overview, and Objectives will be woefully inadequate. The 30 minutes currently allocated are sufficient only to introduce the workshop objectives, to introduce the participants to each other if they are not already acquainted, and to discuss the purposes for which research is done. Discussion of the purposes and motives behind research can be an interesting and worthwhile activity, and it could consume four hours easily. In conducting a workshop, therefore, it makes sense to deal with concerns about purpose and motive, but only long enough to bring a clear focus to the discussion. The workshop concerns issues that are common to both research and implementation.

Group size is an important problem. The workshop will run best with about 10 to 12 people. And the group should not be smaller than six, not larger than twenty. Diversity of experience and opinion is desirable and there should be plenty of "air time" for each participant.

The workshop itself should be structured to address both cognitive and behavioral aspects of designing research and implementation. After the introduction and review of the objectives, as well as clarifying the purpose of the workshop (to focus on research for implementation, not research for other purposes), the Comp Graf case should be discussed. The case introduces many of the factors in real situations, some of them quite subtle, which influence the effectiveness of research and implementation. Comp Graf does not exist. The case was synthesized to represent many different critical incidents, and you will find many participants in your group who will recognize various characters or situations ("I know a guy just like George Simon"). See Appendix B for suggestions on using the case.

The Comp Graf case provides the basis for a cognitive awareness of designing research and implementation in the real world.

In the second phase of the workshop, this awareness is reinforced at the behavioral level, with up to four role plays and discussions concerning implementation skills. Setting up, observing, and analyzing each of the role plays will take a minimum of 45 minutes each and an hour would be highly desirable. The first three role plays should be done in front of the whole group and in the fourth, each participant should use his or her own scenario, prepared in advance of the workshop, and play one of the roles in it. This would be done in small groups of three people each.

The purpose of doing the role plays is to bring research and implementation to a specific behavioral pragmatic level. There is a world of difference between understanding a principle and putting that principle into action. This second segment focuses on action.

You may find some among your participants who object to having to "sell" their ideas. Use the objections as an opportunity for demonstrating your effective implementation skills and listen openly. The Learning Points furnished to all participants in Chapter 5 contain many suggestions about how to handle such a situation. Participant concerns about selling represent a generic problem in gaining cooperation for research. Your influence as a model will be very important.

Speaking about modeling, if this workshop is to be offered as part of a course, done a few hours at a time over the duration of a quarter or a semester, it would be worth investing the time and effort to create a series of modeling displays or films or videotapes to illustrate the learning points.

The role plays will raise even more issues than were on the table at the conclusion of the Comp Graf case. The final segment of the workshop presents the heroic challenge of bringing all these issues together and of trying to achieve some closure. If the workshop is done in a single day, three or four dominant themes are likely to emerge. Like it or not, the discussion will probably focus on them. There is no outline for this session because there are so many different possibilities of what can be done. There is no way to fit everything into the available time. For example, discussion time might be devoted to analysis and discussion of the Research Style Inventory and its right and wrong answers. Or it might be spent on obscurities of academic research such as quantitative analysis and verbal fog as epitomized in the Interpretation Guide for the Research Style Inventory. Time might be spent in a large group or small groups might plan an actual implementation program concerning stress at Comp Graf. Time might be spent in creating a model of the research process in the real world and contrasting it with the traditional hypothetical-deductive method. Other possibilities will arise as you go along.

Regardless of which combination of activities you use, at the end of the workshop you will need to make some summarizing and concluding statement, an act that is needed to provide at least a feeling of closure, even if none has really been achieved. Chapter 6 includes a list of "Critical Factors Relating to Successful Implementation Efforts." People will have read it, but perhaps perfunctorily. It makes a good outline for your concluding remarks.

Appendix B
Teaching Note for the Comp Graf Case

Michael Beer

INTRODUCTION

The purpose of this case is to allow students to diagnose the strategy and tactics of a researcher engaged in research with implementation in mind. In doing so, students can become acquainted with major issues that must be considered when approaching an applied research problem in which action on the part of managers is the intended outcome. The situation chosen purposely involves a researcher who has dual motives. His or her academic training predisposes him or her to contributing to knowledge and to conducting research that adheres to standards of research design commonly taught in graduate programs of organizational behavior or psychology. But, his or her goal to implement results calls for an organic research process that involves managers. These dual objectives pose a dilemma and ultimately lead to the problems George Simon, the researcher, faces. It is assumed that the goal of implementation is both valid and important. Thus, simply saying that the researcher's mistake was to make implementation an objective is not a sufficient response to the case, although it is one that some students might make.

The case is a composite of several actual reports of research with implementation goals. In all of these reports the researchers either failed to obtain entry into the organization, or, if they did, failed in their objectives for implementation. An analysis of these reports revealed that there are many commonalities in these failure experiences, such as the researcher's primary motivation to contribute to knowledge in a form acceptable to the academic community, the assumption that contributing to knowledge means adhering to traditional research methods, assumptions that research subjects cannot be involved in the research for fear of biasing them, and assumptions that managers who express support for research are ready to act on results. Failures also occur because researchers lack skills in entering an organization, contracting for implementation, and managing a process of research that leads to ownership of findings and commitment to act.

The research topic of managerial stress was chosen because it can be analyzed at both the individual and organizational levels. The latter focus requires an organizational perspective so often lacking in industrial/organizational psychology. It highlights the fact that the organizational context must be changed if stress is to be reduced. It therefore presents a more difficult implementation problem than simply putting in a different selection or training program, though these may also be legitimate action alternatives. An article by Ivancevich and Matteson (1980) presents this perspective quite nicely and provides a conceptual framework that allows students to grapple with alternative research designs (to the one used in the case) that might have led to more commitment by management to implement.

The setting, a rapidly growing high technology company, is based on another case, but has been modified a little based on experience in several other rapidly growing high technology companies. If the instructor chooses to tell students that this case is a composite of several situations, he or she can assure students that both the organization and the researcher's experience are quite realistic. All participants at the Innovation in Methodology Conference found the case credible and an accurate representation of their own applied research experience.

ASSUMPTIONS

My underlying assumption is that research with implementation in mind requires a very different outlook on the part of the researcher than research that does not have action objectives. The researcher must be concerned about the motivation of the client or research subjects to provide valid data and to act on the conclusions of the research. Assessing client motivation and/or developing it through involving employees and managers therefore becomes very important. Similarly, the perceived relevance of the research questions, instruments, and process become as important as scientific rigor. While client motivation and involvement and scientific rigor (defined in traditional terms) are not necessarily mutually exclusive, in many instances rigor can only be obtained at a cost to involvement. This is because traditional scientific methods typically call for more distance between the researcher and the client and more control over the research process by the researcher than by the client. The conflict between rigor and client motivation represents a major dilemma that a researcher with implementation in mind must manage.

There are some conceptual frameworks and ideas that can be very helpful to researchers seeking implementation of research findings. These ideas are associated with the fields of organization development, action research, and intervention theory and method (see reference list). For example, effectiveness in managing research with implementation in mind involves skills in diagnosing one's own motivation as a researcher and the client's motivation, and it requires skills in making strategic and tactical choices in entry, contracting, and implementation. These choices are situationally determined and hence require skills in situational diagnosis and responsive research planning. The case acquaints students with the values, conceptual issues, and tactical skills and thought processes that surround research with implementation in mind. Some skill development is possible through having students role play various critical interactions in the case. The behavior modeling and role-play exercises that go along with this case are designed for more extensive skill development opportunities than the case provides.

The Comp Graf case raises the following issues typically faced by researchers whose goals are implementation.

(1) The problem of motivation and commitment to the research as a fundamental ingredient in implementing research findings. How do you identify whether motivation exists or how do you develop it?

(2) The problem of multiple constituencies and interest groups with respect to the research. How do you deal with these at the entry stage to ensure their cooperation at the implementation stage?

(3) The problem of researcher neutrality in power struggles of political constituencies. Can the researcher establish rapport with all constituencies? What mechanism might be chosen to do so?

(4) The appropriate role for the researcher when he or she enters the organization. Does he or she view him- or herself strictly as a researcher or does he or she recognize the need to develop consensus and commitment to act in advance of the data collection phase? Is he or she therefore willing to sacrifice immediate research goals to obtain long-term implementation success? Is the researcher willing to confront issues early?

(5) The issue of research methodology. Is the researcher willing to give up control over design and method as well as some rigor to obtain commitment?

(6) The issue of researcher credibility. Is the researcher able to present him- or herself as a credible person with not only technical competence but managerial savvy?

(7) The problem of multiple hierarchical levels. Is the researcher able to reestablish commitment to the research at levels below the top where the initial contact is made? What mechanisms of introduction and communication are chosen?

(8) Reading signals that problems are developing that may prevent implementation. What tactics can the researcher use and when should he or she cut losses?

(9) The issue of theory-based versus problems-centered research. Is the researcher willing to change the focus of research so it is more aligned with the organization's real problems?

(10) The problem of lag between initiation of research and feedback of results. What can the researcher do to shorten this time (implication for method) and what can he or she do to bridge the lag and keep management involved?

(11) The problem of shifting circumstances. How can the researcher prevent his or her research focus from becoming obsolete?

(12) The problem of feedback. When, how, where, who, and what?

(13) The problem for the researcher of understanding the business sufficiently to make the research relevant and the recommendations realistic.

(14) Managing the expectations of management for the research. How to keep these expectations sufficiently high to gain interest and sufficiently low to be realistic.

CASE ANALYSIS

THE RESEARCHER

George Simon is typical of many academics with his background and orientation. He would like implementation, but his stronger motive is contribution to knowledge and publication of results in a refereed journal. Recognizing in oneself the importance of this goal and the extent to which it will dominate decisions about research design and process is key to understanding why we often fail to achieve the best of intentions for implementation. Even industrial researchers, for whom publication is less important, fall prey to the traditions of "normal science" ingrained in them while they are graduate students. George Simon starts with many assumptions about research design and the role this imposes on him and the research subjects that make it hard for him to see other alternatives. The fact that this research is part of a program for which standardized questionnaires and data have already been developed simply compounds his problems.

THE COMPANY AND BUSINESS

Like George Simon, many researchers simply do not understand organizations or business sufficiently to appreciate what is going on. This lack of knowledge prevents George Simon from appreciating the contextual factors at Comp Graf that cause stress and the problem he will have in getting management to act on the stress problems. Thus, the case allows students to practice these skills, should that be a learning objective. The problems we see are typical of high technology, rapid growth firms. The following are the key factors in the situation that George Simon should have perceived and understood.

(1) *Business Environment*

- The business is growing at 50 percent a year with attendant changes in tasks, roles, and demands.

- Requirements for capital to finance growth put pressures on profits and make the order backlog particularly important.

- It is a highly competitive business with rapid changes in market and products.

- There is a constant requirement for new products and more advanced technology that perform the same function more efficiently and less expensively. The development of new products demands coordination between functions (marketing, manufacturing, and engineering).

(2) *Business and Human Outcomes*

- The sales forecast of $125 million versus $140 million and the drop in order backlog is an important business fact that should warn Simon of impending pressures on the business.

- High personnel turnover puts additional stress on management and employees whose competencies and energies are already stretched.

- High levels of personal stress are expressed from the president on down. ("People put out 150 percent.") There is no one to go to up the line for help and support. The result is high levels of pressure.

(3) *Structures and Systems*

- Separate buildings for the functions contributes to poor integration between functions.

- Marketing has product/business managers who are responsible for profits of their product lines. To achieve profits and growth they must obtain the cooperation of people in other functions who do not report to them. This matrix structure may be required, but it creates ambiguity in roles and relationships, and requires skills managers do not have. All this contributes to stress.

(4) *Management Process and Style*

Interviews conducted by Simon later (too late) in the research process indicate a number of problems in the management process of the firm. These problems are a function of the stage of development of the firm, poor management skills and ineffective management by McMulty.

- There is a *low level of trust* between functions and a lot of inter-functional conflict. This, of course, leads to poor coordination between marketing, engineering, and manufacturing. Coordination is needed to solve problems and to be responsive to market demands for price, products, and service.

- There is a *lack of coordinate planning* at the top. Marketing's view of the market place is never properly communicated and integrated into a view of what should be done. This leads to surprises and consequent negative views of marketing. However, the problem may not be marketing's competence but a lack of communication and joint planning.

- McMulty makes decisions *without involving the functional heads* and then reverses decisions without involving them. The result is confusion and resentment.

- *Lack of delegation* results in overload at the top and lack of management development in the middle. Lack of management competence in the middle prevents top management from delegating. It is a vicious cycle.

- McMulty is an engineer, scientist, and inventor, *not a manager*. He apparently does not want to or does not have the skill to pull his team together in a coordinated effort. He lets them operate on their own and does not confront them to get coordinated action. Most meetings are one to one. Meetings that they do have are for information sharing, not for problem solving and planning.

(5) *People*

- The continual *shortage of people* means that everyone is working long hours. Time spent on recruiting takes precious time away from running the business, further hurting effectiveness.

- Rapid growth constantly creates *new demands* on people. The need to grow into these new jobs is a major source of stress. The inability of managers to develop new competencies causes ineffectiveness, itself a cause of stress.

- The inability of some managers to grow requires that they be moved aside if the business is to survive. Dealing with these personal problems means breaking old relationships and is stressful. If they are not dealt with, frustration with poor performance is still stressful.

- Many of the key people are engineers. Their technical training has created the business, but their lack of managerial skills is contributing to current problems.

(6) *Culture*

The total effect of these factors is an organizational culture characterized by informality, no rules, ambiguity, controlled chaos, flexibility, "go it alone to make it happen," rapid change, and little planning. Essentially, people perceive that the norm is for individuals and departments to fight fires, take action, and be responsive without coordinated planning with others.

The above analysis indicates that a program of stress management will have to deal with all these root causes. Indeed, it suggests that to reduce stress, management may have to ask itself if it can continue to grow as rapidly as it is currently doing. If this question is to be addressed, the stage must be properly set by Simon at entry.

THE ENTRY AND RESEARCH-
PLANNING PROCESS

A major part of the case discussion should center around an analysis of the research process. What were George Simon's communications, interactions, agreements, and decisions from initial introduction at Comp Graf to the data feedback process? What did he do that contributed to the problems we see and what might have been done differently? In effect, what were the critical points in the project's life at which different choices might have resulted in different outcomes? By taking students through the research project from beginning to end, a complete analysis of all these choice points is made possible.

(1) *Initial Contact*

- Simon's initial contact is with Rick Long, the personnel manager. While this is a perfectly legitimate way to make initial contact, the researcher must be cautious about the enthusiasm of a staff specialist. Does it reflect line management's views? Are they enthusiastic?

- Did Simon become too enthusiastic as a result of Long's statement that Jones, the marketing manager, was enthusiastic?

- Early assumptions about the enthusiasm of managers for a research project can blind one to pitfalls that need to be identified and dealt with.

(2) *Initial Visit*

- Simon notices the informal nature of the company when he first enters the front door. This is a clue about the culture that should inform his diagnosis and plans for entry.

- Simon's initial discussions with Jones, the marketing manager, and his open acceptance of Jones's support, actually hurt Simon later on. His association with Jones aligns him "with Jones" in the conflict between marketing and the other functions and may be responsible for the attacks on Simon by Bertram, the vice president of manufacturing. Researchers should not openly accept the support of any group until they understand the group's power and role in the organization. In this case, marketing is at the center of many problems and is under attack. Their central role in coordination and product management makes this inevitable. Jones's enthusiasm for the stress research is in part a reflection of the pressure on marketing. He may be using the research to bolster his position or to put pressure on McMulty, the president, whom he sees as the problem.

- Simon feels uncomfortable with Jones' support, but does not pay attention to this internal signal and its meaning.

- Simon's presentation of his research objectives (page 76) is a tip off about Simon's mind set. His first three points deal with knowledge, theory, and data. Only his last point deals with implementation. A research project with implementation goals must start with implementation as a primary goal. Everything else including contributions to knowledge and theory emerge from a research process designed to obtain commitment and action. This is of course contrary to research design dictums which emphasize scientific rigor.

(3) *Meeting with McMulty the President*

Simon's first meeting with McMulty was full of signals about Comp Graf, McMulty the manager, and about McMulty's motivation to become involved in the research. These should have informed Simon's tactics in entering the organization and designing a research strategy and process. Instead, Simon seems not to notice, confront issues, or modify his research strategy.

- There were delays in the meeting with McMulty. Simon should at least have asked what these meant about commitment and about the organization.

- Once in McMulty's office, the meeting was interrupted several times. This is an indicator of McMulty's management style and the relationship of that style to stress in the organization. It is also an indicator of McMulty's potential skills in implementing a program to reduce stress.

- The computer terminal in his office simply reinforces that McMulty is primarily a technical man, not a manager.

- Simon starts the meeting with McMulty by outlining his research objectives, leaving implementation as the last item. This means that *he* is defining the problem and the project. With implementation of research findings as the goal, Simon might have been better off asking McMulty to define what problems led him to be interested in the stress research. This would have been a good way to diagnose readiness to implement a program of stress management and/or it could have further developed such readiness.

- McMulty's mention of personal pressure and his personal concerns about life style (time with family) are a warning that he may be interested in the research for personal reasons but not as a manager concerned with employees' stress and organizational effectiveness. The latter concern is probably needed if he is to take a leadership role in implementing research findings. Simon misses this signal completely.

- Simon assumes that McMulty's personal interest is sufficient backing to ensure implementation. He never asks McMulty about whether he and his staff have reached consensus about the importance of stress management as a goal for improvement.

- Simon never tries to find a link between stress management and business problems at Comp Graf. Nor is he concerned that McMulty does not ask about that link. The result is a research project perceived by Bertram, the manufacturing vice president, as contributing nothing to improving organizational effectivenss. In fact, many of the causes of stress are also causes of ineffectiveness.

(4) *Meeting with McMulty's Staff*

There were a number of problems in the way Simon approached and conducted the meeting with McMulty's staff. This is a key meeting that influences perceptions of Simon by key power figures and sets the direction for the rest of the project.

- Simon does not meet with all the individuals on McMulty's staff individually prior to the meeting. Such a preparatory step would have given Simon a lot of information about their interests in the problem of stress, established relationships with them, established his neutrality, and informed Simon about the organization. Without these meetings Simon has no way to evaluate the potential effect on his research of Jones's open support. This is important since this support probably associates the research with marketing, a function already under fire. Additionally, prior meetings may have answered questions about research financing from the vice president of finance or prevented attacks by the vice president of manufacturing.

- Simon never takes notice of the fact that the greeting by Jones and Jones's support of the stress research makes the other managers ill at ease. Reading signals can allow corrective action.

- Simon does not involve himself with McMulty in planning the meeting. Thus, there are managers there he does not know or expect. Furthermore, Simon does not obtain a commitment from McMulty to introduce him at the meeting. Long ends up doing that, signaling to McMulty's staff that the research is not that important after all.

- McMulty's statement that he prefers not to attend the first meeting because he does not want to pressure his staff is an indication that McMulty may not be counted on for strong leadership of the research and implementation process. Had Simon understood the meaning of the statement he might have been able to help McNulty see the need for leadership or, alternatively, he might have withdrawn.

- Simon and his assistant choose to present the details of their research design, method, and questionnaire instead of asking McMulty's staff to discuss business and stress problems they perceive. Thus, consensus about the problem to be researched and commitment to implementation is not developed. Presenting a predetermined approach to the research clearly makes it Simon's research, not management's.

- Simon and his assistant fall back on questionnaire standardization as a rationale for not involving managers in questionnaire design. The result is still further loss of commitment.

- That there is little active discussion at the meeting, and the attack by the vice president of manufacturing is not seen by Simon as a warning that things are going off track.

- McMulty's statement after the meeting that his managers might have supported the research if they had talked to Simon individually merely reinforces the fact that these one-to-one discussions should have taken place prior to the meeting.

- The reported reaction of key managers to Simon's "academic" presentation should clearly have signaled that there was a need to rethink the whole approach to research if implementation was to be achieved.

(5) *Meetings with Key Personnel*

The interviews with key personnel at Comp Graf (see earlier analysis of organizational problems) provide rich data about problems that should have informed Simon about the issues of concern to management. Many of these are, of course, related to stress. The interviews should have been seen as an important data-gathering step in the research, one that could inform the research design and later data-gathering steps. Instead, Simon views the research as the questionnaire and the interviews as a necessary step to administer it.

CONDUCTING THE RESEARCH

The interview findings could have been shared by Simon with McMulty. That feedback to McMulty and later to his staff could have led to joint planning of the research and greater commitment to action. Instead, Simon continues to ignore signals that management is not committed to the research or to implementation.

(1) *The Questionnaire*

- Simon does modify the questionnaire to include items based on interview findings, a small but insufficient step to obtain commitment. In the end the questionnaire is too long (250 items).

- The questionnaire is pretested.

- But it took two months to redesign the questionnaire. This delay causes a further loss of momentum.

(2) *Preparation Meetings*

- The meetings to inform people about the research are large.

- The researchers do deal with the confidentiality issue.

- But the researchers follow traditional research wisdom by being vague about the purpose of the research and about their plans for feedback. Keeping subjects in the dark may prevent bias but it also prevents Simon from motivating employees to provide valid data.

(3) *Questionnaire Administration and Analysis*

It could be argued that by this time Simon has passed the point of no return in salvaging this project as implementation research. Nevertheless, several of the questionnaire administration and analysis procedures represent typical problems found in research designed with implementation in mind.

- Questionnaires are filled out at home not at work.

- Objection by vice presidents about giving work time to questionnaire administration is just one more comfirmation that there is no commitment.

- The computer analysis takes three months, is too complex for feedback purposes, and distances the researcher from the organization.

DATA FEEDBACK

Many aspects of the feedback process preclude developing commitment to the research findings. An analysis of these by students can help them appreciate the issues that must be considered in designing an effective feedback process. Furthermore, just before the feedback process begins, Long reports that there are problems with new product developments. The irony is that much of the data Simon collected in interviews, if they had been seen as legitimate and utilized, could have helped management deal with these problems and with stress.

(1) *Feedback to Top Management*

- The data were not fed back to McMulty first.

- McMulty did not chair the feedback meeting. This is necessary to signal commitment to implementation.

- Aggregate corporate data are presented. There is no breakdown of how the top group responded.

- The analysis presented is far too sophisticated for managers to understand or to be useful to them in considering action.

- The data are not presented in a way relevant to the business concerns of management. This angers the vice president of manufacturing, who is under performance pressure. Simon does not respond by showing how the data is relevant to current business problems.

- Jones's support of the research findings and his use of them to support his position against other functions leads to conflict. The outburst by Ardmore puts new data on the table about problems at Comp Graf that cause poor performance and stress. But Simon lacks the vision or skill to grasp an opportunity to get a meaningful discussion going.

- A discussion of problems does finally develop. McMulty suggests that perhaps rapid growth is the villain. But Simon does not know how to mobilize the group to see how their decision to grow rapidly is at the core of many of their problems, including stress.

- The final indicator of impending failure is the attack on the data by the managers.

(2) *Feedback to Functional Groups*

By the time feedback to the functional departments occurs, it is already too late. Nevertheless, further problems arise from which students can learn.

- The manufacturing department does not request feedback. This is not surprising given the attitude of the vice president of manufacturing. His commitment was lost long ago.

- The meetings are too large and prevent open candid discussion and problem solving.

- Aggregate corporate data are presented rather than a breakdown of data by the department receiving the feedback. This makes the data less relevant as evidenced by requests for such data.

- There are questions about commitment at the top. Given the lack of commitment developed there, Simon cannot reassure people, removing any last chance for meaningful implementation at lower levels.

- The meetings degenerate into disagreements about items and data. When this happens, the process of research and feedback fails to obtain commitment.

REFLECTIONS ON WHAT TO DO NOW

The case ends with the question of whether Simon should work with Jones, who is the only one interested in implementation. Given the systemic nature of the problems and the conflict between marketing and other functions, can an effort with Jones's department lead to meaningful changes that will reduce stress in marketing? Can Simon salvage anything from this mess?

TEACHING PLAN

TEACHING BY THE CASE METHOD

A case provides students the opportunity to put themselves into a real-life situation in which they are called on for analysis and decisions. To prepare for a case discussion students must read the case before class and come prepared to discuss their analysis of the situation and their view of what the principle character should have done or should do now. To aid students in their preparation, the instructor provides students with preparation questions to be discussed in class. Written answers to these questions are not required or even desirable, though students should have notes to aid them in the class discussion.

The instructor's role in class is to orchestrate a discussion of the case. The instructor may lead off with an analysis question (Why did George Simon fail in his efforts to have his research findings implemented?) or with an action question (What should George Simon do now? What could Simon have done differently?). The instructor then solicits students' views on these questions, recording key comments or the outline of an action plan on the blackboard. As many students as possible should be brought into the discussion, and they should be encouraged to build on each other's answers or to disagree with each other. As the discussion progresses, a composite analysis or action plan emerges that is richer than that of any individual student. The instructor can keep the discussion moving by asking follow-up questions aimed at moving the discussion into areas of analysis or action that pose a particular puzzle or dilemma. For example, what caused the difficulties Simon experienced in the meeting with McMulty and his key managers? What could he have done differently? Why was it difficult for Simon to see the need to change his research design as resistance developed? How might he have changed the research design? The discussion may also be directed to deal with broader issues that the case raises. For example, what are the implications of this case for research methodology when implementation of findings is a goal? Are the objectives of implementation and contribution to knowledge incompatible?

The discussion need not proceed in an orderly fashion and usually does not. A good discussion moves fairly rapidly from one student to another. At various points the instructor may summarize or pose a new question. In this fashion the instructor moves the discussion to new areas of interest that he or she has determined through his or her own analysis to be key learning points. For this reason, it is very important that the instructor has read the case, prepared his or her own analysis of it, and decided on key learning points. The case analysis in the previous section of this teaching note has been provided to help instructors with their own analyses.

There are alternatives to a discussion of a case by the whole class. Students may be asked to discuss certain questions in small groups and to report to the larger class about key conclusions or issues discussed. Sometimes, such small discussion groups may be used to prepare students for a larger class discussion and sometimes they may be the primary forum for learning. Students may also be asked to submit written reports containing their analyses or action plans. Students can also be asked to make a presentation of their individual or group reports.

TEACHING PLAN FOR COMP GRAF

The Comp Graf case lends itself to an analysis of why Simon's goal for implementation of research findings failed and what he could have done differently at each phase of the research process. The case also provides an opportunity for students to analyze the data about Comp Graf and to suggest approaches to interventions or action research that might have been more successful in reducing stress, while at the same time, resulting in a contribution to knowledge. The article by Ivancevich and Matteson (1980) provides background on stress management (to be read along with the case before class) that should allow students to analyze the causes of stress at Comp Graf and to discuss alternative research interventions.

I suggest that the class discussion proceed through the following sequence of questions and discussion segments. The outline assumes an hour-and-a-half class.

(1) *Why was Simon unsuccessful in getting management to implement a stress prevention or management program based on his research findings?* The instructor can simply list on the black-

board major reasons given. This is a warm-up for the next phase of the discussion (15 minutes).

(2) *Let's analyze the whole research process from beginning to end, identifying key places at which problems arose and alternative actions Simon might have taken. How did it all start?* In this discussion the instructor will want to take students through a more rigorous analysis of each step taken by Simon from first contact with Long (the personnel manager) through entry, initial meetings, data collection and feedback (see analysis in previous section). The key steps in the research process may be listed on the blackboard in advance or students can be asked to identify them as the discussion progresses. As each point is listed, students are asked, "What was the problem here? To what should Simon have been sensitive? What should he have done differently? (35 minutes).

(3) *Given what you have learned about Comp Graf from the case and about stress from the article, what alternative data collection interventions might have resulted in implementation and a contribution to knowledge?* Students should be asked to suggest means of data collection that might be perceived as more relevant by executives and that would involve them more in the research process. In particular students should be encouraged to see the potential in a sequence of data collection steps starting with a discussion of problems with McMulty and his staff, followed by a preliminary definition of problems by that group, moving to preliminary interviews, feedback to top management of findings and agreement by them on research questions to be asked, and ending in a broader data collection (interviews or questionnaires) and feedback phase (25 minutes).

(4) *The last part of class should be reserved for a summary.* The instructor may provide that summary or ask students to step back from the case and arrive at generalizations. What generalizations do you draw from this case discussion? What are the implications of the case for research in which both implementation and contribution to knowledge are the goal? (15 minutes)

The teaching plan outlined here may be modified in a number of ways. For example, analysis of the case, discussion of an alternative approach to research, and generalizations about research with implementation in mind could each be separate classes, with assigned readings about research with implementation in mind as background for the last two classes (see references).

References

Alderfer, C. P. The methodology of organizational diagnosis. *Professional Psychology*, 1979.

Argyris, C. Some unintended consequences of rigorous research. *Psychological Bulletin*, 1968, 70, 185-197.

Argyris, C. *Intervention theory and method: A behavioral science view*. Reading, MA: Addison-Wesley, 1970.

Argyris, C. *Inner contradictions of rigorous research*. New York: Academic Press, 1980.

Beer, M. *Organizational change and development: A systems view*. Santa Monica, CA: Goodyear, 1981.

Ivancevich, J. M., & Matteson, M. T. Optimizing human resources: A case for preventive health and stress management. *Organizational Dynamics*, 1980, 9, 5-25.

Komaki, J., Barwick, K. D., & Scott, L. R. A behavioral approach to occupational safety: Pinpointing and reinforcing safe performance in a food manufacturing plant. *Journal of Applied Psychology*, 1978, 63, 434-445.

Kotter, J. P. *The general manager*. New York: Free Press, 1982.

Levinson, H. *Organizational diagnosis*. Cambridge, MA: Harvard University Press, 1972.

Lindblom, C. E., & Cohen, D. K. *Useable knowledge: Social science and social problem solving*. New Haven, CT: Yale University Press, 1979.

McCall, M. *Leadership as a design problem*. Technical Report 5. Greensboro, NC: Center for Creative Leadership, 1978.

McCaskey, M. G. The hidden messages managers send. *Harvard Business Review*, 1979, 57(6), 135-148.

Middleton, T. Light refractions—dissertationese. *Saturday Review*, January 19, 1980.

Mintzberg, H. *The nature of managerial work*. New York: Harper & Row, 1973.

Mintzberg, H. Organizational design: Fashion or fit. *Harvard Business Review*, 1981, 59, 103-116.

Peters, T. J. Putting excellence into management. *Business Week*, July 21, 1980.

Pettigrew, A. M. The influence process between specialists and executives. *Personnel Review*, 1974, 3, 5.

Sayles, L. R. Managing on the run. *Executive*, 1980, 6(3), 25-26.

Schneider, B. The service organization: Climate is crucial. *Organizational Dynamics*, 1980, 9, 52-65.

About the Authors

MILTON D. HAKEL, Ph.D., is Professor of Psychology at the Ohio State University. He is the editor of *Personnel Psychology,* and also serves as President of Organizational Research and Development, Inc., a consulting company in Columbus, Ohio. A Fellow and member of the Executive Committee of the Society for Industrial and Organizational Psychology (Division 14) of the American Psychological Association (APA), he has recently been elected to the APA Board of Professional Affairs and to the Board of Trustees of the Association for the Advancement of Psychology. He received the James McKeen Cattell Award given by Division 14 for excellence in research design and is a former Fulbright-Hays Senior Scholar.

MELVIN SORCHER, Ph.D., is Director of Management Development for Richardson-Vicks, in Wilton, Connecticut. Prior to that, he was Manager of Personnel Research at General Electric, where he developed behavior modeling for use in industrial and nonclinical situations. Division 14 of the American Psychological Association awarded him the Professional Practice Award for that work. He is a Fellow of the Society for Industrial and Organizational Psychology of the American Psychological Association. He is the author, with A. Goldstein, of *Changing Supervisor Behavior.*

MICHAEL BEER, Ph.D., is Professor of Business Administration at Harvard University. He was formerly the Director of Organizational Research and Development at Corning Glass Works. He is a Fellow of the Society for Industrial and Organizational Psychology of the American Psychological Association. A consultant to industry, he is also the author of *Organizational Change and Development: A Systems View* (1980).

JOSEPH L. MOSES, Ph.D., is Manager of Personnel Research at American Telephone and Telegraph, Morristown, New Jersey. He also serves as Research Professor at New York University. A Fellow of the Society for Industrial and Organizational Psychology of the American Psychological Association (Division 14), he is also a Diplomate of the American Board of Professional Psychology. Joel is the author, with William Byham, of *Applying the Assessment Center Method.*